Kylie — you

The
Master
Empath?

TURNING ON YOUR EMPATH GIFTS AT WILL

— IN LOVE, BUSINESS AND FRIENDSHIP

(Includes Training In Skilled Empath Merge)

YES ,

Rose Rosetree

— Rose

Women's Intuition Worldwide
Sterling, Virginia

The Master Empath

TURNING ON YOUR EMPATH GIFTS AT WILL

— IN LOVE, BUSINESS AND FRIENDSHIP

(Includes Training In Skilled Empath Merge)

Empath Empowerment® with Rose Rosetree, Series Book Three. Empath Empowerment® is Rose Rosetree's unique system for helping empaths to improve quality of life, using techniques for appropriate positioning of consciousness, a system to help people born with one or more gifts as an empath.

This book includes many techniques for Skilled Empath Merge. These techniques move awareness in ways that are subtle yet powerful. Never do any technique for Skilled Empath Merge while operating machinery or driving a car. Allow 30 minutes after doing a Skilled Empath Merge before you start doing any of those things, either, just to be on the safe side. The information in this book has been researched over many years.

The author and publisher assume no liability whatsoever for damages of any kind that occur directly or indirectly from the use of statements in this book. You alone are responsible for how you use the information here.

PUBLISHER'S CATALOGING-IN-PUBLICATION

Rosetree, Rose.

The master empath : turning on your empath gifts at will — in love, business and friendship : (includes training in Skilled Empath Merge) / Rose Rosetree.

Empowered empath : owning, embracing and managing your gifts / Rose Rosetree.

To come pages ; 14 x 21.59 centimeters cm. — (An Empath Empowerment® Books series ; book 3)

Includes bibliographical references and index in an online supplement.

Issued also as an ebook.

ISBN-13: 978-1-935214-33-5
ISBN-10: 1-935214-33-0

1. Empathy. 2. Intuition. 3. Sensitivity (Personality trait) 4. Self-actualization (Psychology)
5. Aura. 6. Self-help techniques. 7. Consciousness. I. Adaptation of (work) Rosetree, Rose.
Empowered by empathy, 25 ways to fly in spirit. II. Title.

BF575.E55 R67 2014   158/.2

ISBN: 978-1-935214-33-5

LCCN: 2014939380

Please direct all correspondence and inquiries to

Women's Intuition Worldwide, LLC
116 Hillsdale Drive, Sterling, VA 20164-1201
rights@rose-rosetree.com
703-450-9514

Visit our website: www.rose-rosetree.com

Dedication

Poets, singers, artists:
you who yearn to express the truth
and yet more truth, open now
to the ways you already create and create without ceasing
through your spirit's gifts.
Dancers, actors, musicians, photographers,
creators of all kinds and intensities:
you who fervently wish that someone, that enough someones,
might give you the chance to show your talent,
open now and be refreshed.
Once upon this time, right here, in this room,
know that wherever you are, you send out your gifts
and applause for them shakes in the air
like the sound right before thunder.

Because you move as an empath,
you are an awakener,
not only through the skills that you cherish
but in all the ways that you serve, bringing light to this world
on a silver(though invisible) platter.

Even you, the hidden ones,
you who keep your gifts secret,
even you whose gifts are kept so far secret
that you do not know them yet,
stop holding back your tears.
Hear the call.
Awaken to the mystery of all you can know
and all that you share,
for our world, like you, is ready to break wide open
and show forth the full joy of God.

Table of Contents

Online Supplement at www.rose-rosetree.com

Glossary — Recommended Reading — Index

Energetic Workarounds
and Techniques

What is an ENERGETIC WORKAROUND? It is a significant way to overcome problems.

By comparison, tips and coping methods are more superficial. A fully realized energetic workaround will re-orient your awareness, causing you to use your empath gifts more effectively. An energetic workaround can even change your life.

Admittedly an energetic *workaround* designed to help empaths is less powerful than a dedicated *technique* for empaths, which holds the power to transport and transform your consciousness.

To clarify the difference, here's an analogy. Imagine that you are working on a project with your computer. Something doesn't go quite right. Again and again you try to make that software work. It just won't.

- ✑ A tip, or coping method, might be to call a help desk.

- ✑ For a workaround, you would take a different approach to solving your problem, maybe do something unusual with the software. Unusual but, hey, it works. Besides, there are no ill effects.

- ✑ A technique would be more like going into the computer software; finding the buggy code and fixing it. Or you might read and follow technical instructions from an expert. Thus you overcome a problem for keeps.

Awakening Empath, I have focused for years on developing expertise about consciousness and how to systematically develop consciousness-related, practical skills like Empath Empowerment®. In general, I'm no big fan of coping strategies or tips. However, I do believe in the power of a well-constructed workaround. I'm glad to share a number of them with you here, in addition to dedicated techniques.

1. *I Want To Hold Your Hand.* My favorite technique for Skilled Empath Merge. — CHAPTERS 4-6.

2. *Deep Listening.* Gain insight by exploring your partner's Heart Chakra. — CHAPTER 7.

3. *Emergency Disconnect from Skilled Empath Merge.* Energy hygiene on demand. — CHAPTER 7.

4. *Find Your Truth Sight Research Tool.* Thanks to this technique, you'll never need glasses for 20-20 wisdom. — CHAPTER 8.

5. *Shallow Up Quickie.* Such an easy energetic workaround for positioning consciousness back at regular, human frequencies! — CHAPTER 8.

6. *Self-Discovery with Truth Sight.* You don't need a magic mirror from Hogwarts to have fun with this. — CHAPTER 9.

7. *Another Super-Easy Way to Turn Empath Gifts OFF.* Here's a fabulously effective energy workaround you can use just about anywhere in the world. — CHAPTER 9.

8. *Truth Sight For Advanced Empath Merge.* This visual technique provides quick entry into the experience of being your chosen "Discovery Person." — CHAPTER 10.

9. *Incognito Truth Sight.* Purposely initiate skilled empath merge with just about anyone who is in the room with you. — CHAPTER 11.

10. *Truth Sight for TV.* An amazing form of Remote Empath Merge that piggybacks on your prior experience at watching television. — CHAPTER 13.

11. *Locate A Handy Tool For Remote Empath Merge.* Learn one more technical skill to help you become a Master Empath. — CHAPTER 14.

12. *Truth-Touching Empath Merge with TV.* And you thought that, previously, you saw something on TV that touched you? Ha, surfacey by comparison! — CHAPTER 15.

PART ONE

Mastery Begins with You

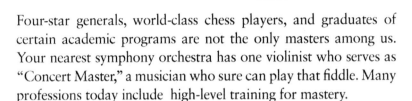

Four-star generals, world-class chess players, and graduates of certain academic programs are not the only masters among us. Your nearest symphony orchestra has one violinist who serves as "Concert Master," a musician who sure can play that fiddle. Many professions today include high-level training for mastery.

What if you become a Master in World of Warcraft? Your status may not be elevated greatly outside your gaming circles. By contrast, legitimate legal categories do exist in America for certain occupations, such as *Master of Swimming Pool Piping* or *Master Electrician.*

Similarly, you can complete this Program for Empath Empowerment and become a Master Empath.

What will that kind of mastery mean?

Here's a comparison. Back in the day, my Grandpa Hugo became a Master Tailor. He grew up in Germany before World War One. Hardworking Hugo lived in a small town that hadn't changed much since the Middle Ages. When he decided to study tailoring, he was apprenticed, then worked as a journeyman.

Eventually Hugo reached a stage of mastery comparable to what you have attained so far in your development as an empath, assuming that you have read *The Empowered Empath.*

When Hugo was ready to learn even more, was required to visit different cities in Europe, studying with the top tailors of his day. Finally Hugo created his masterpiece and earned his guild standing as a Master Tailor.

What does it mean to become a Master Empath? You won't have to buy spools of thread in every conceivable color.

Nor need you travel in person to watch your role models use early-model sewing machines. From the comfort of home, you will travel in consciousness, a.k.a. Mastering techniques for Skilled Empath Merge.

To complete this Program for Empath Empowerment, you will learn to master many variations on Skilled Empath Merge. As for your greatest masterpiece? That will be you.

CHAPTER 1

Awakening into a Stronger Sense of Self

Who are you? That sense of identity you have as a person: Could be, that's where you used to get clobbered.

Back in the day, didn't those unskilled empath merges make it hard to figure out who, exactly, you were? You, of all people.

Developing a SENSE OF IDENTITY means gaining a workable, conscious set of thoughts and feelings about yourself as an individual. What makes you special? Why would people want to get to know you? And who will they meet when they do?

Refining your personal sense of identity can help you to feel safe and whole.

Granted, refining that sense of self can also be tricky. It's a problem for any thoughtful adult, not just empaths. Personal development could even be defined as a quest for identity.

Given your naturally high standards as an empath, exploring identity is an especially big deal. Definitely not as easy as shopping for a new sofa. A workable sense of who-you-be combines abstract, subjective experiences with concrete facts about objective reality:

- Your name
- Your height and weight
- Your age
- Where you live

What, does that have to count as me? That can't be fair!

In his famous speech, "I Have a Dream," Dr. Martin Luther King, Jr. looked forward to a time when human beings would be judged on the content of their character, not the color of their skin.

In reality, none of us has that luxury. To fully appreciate who we are, we must include both skin color and character, plus so much more. Those unskilled empath merges you used to do? They added even more to the mix, more than was workable.

No wonder empath coaching is an emerging field, with more resources available every passing year.

It began with *Empowered by Empathy*, the first book in English for empaths — what would later become the Empath Empowerment series, but in seed form.

You could compare it to Microsoft Windows 95, while *The Empowered Empath* and *The Master Empath* are more comparable to current versions of Word. A lot has happened between 1998 (when I started that first empath's book) and now.

Since 1998, there has been an ever increasing supply of services for empaths, plus books and supoprt groups and other resources. One way to evaluate them is to question whether or not they result in helping an empath to develop a stronger sense of identity.

This system does. Your life is about to improve significantly, even beyond what you have already gained from Empath Empowerment.

Strengthening Your Sense of Self

The Master Empath aims to complete what began with *The Empowered Empath*. Let's review how that prequel helped you to refine your sense of identity. (This survey may bring to mind ways that you have grown already but not yet consciously recognized.)

AWAKENING EMPATH is what I will be calling you, during this survey and afterwards. Thus far into developing empath skills, you have begun to develop a stronger sense of self.

No longer distracted by random flying in spirit, you have gained the freedom to awaken further, pursuing your path of personal growth much faster than ever before.

Altogether, this Program for Empath Empowerment includes three steps. Only two of them are required. Thse steps were taught to you in *The Empowered Empath*, building your self-confidence.

    ∽ Step ONE helped you understand the basics. What does it means to be an empath in general? What are your empath gifts in particular? Which one(s) did you relate to, out of all 15 different gifts? Recognizing any one of these gifts would qualify you to call yourself an empath for life.

    ∽ Step TWO taught you how to develop the habit of keeping your empath gifts turned OFF. Like any simple light switch on a wall, at any given moment your complete set of empath gifts is turned either OFF or ON. For an unskilled empath, the gifts are usually ON. By now, yours are usually OFF. (Hooray!)

    ∽ Step THREE in the Program for Empath Empowerment means learning how to turn your empath gifts ON. Safely. Briefly. Informatively. Intentionally.

Sure, this third step is optional. Yet I think you will find it irresistible, fascinating, and even amazing in a non-dramatic way.

Besides being huge fun, Skilled Empath Merge gives you such an advantage for "Love, Business And Friendship." (What, you had a hunch all that was going to be discussed? It sure will.)

Meanwhile, back at your sense of identity, what difference can it make, completing each of these three steps of empath training? Let's validate about the first two, then preview the third — which happens to be the purpose of this book.

Step ONE. Consciousness-Raising for Empaths

During Step ONE of Empath Empowerment, you began by naming yourself appropriately as an empath. It's pretty hard for any empath to develop a strong sense of identity without effective naming.

Here's a related example. Back in the early days of feminism, Betty Friedan courageously described "The problem that has no name." Her visionary book, published in 1963, was *The Feminine Mystique*. This was the first time an American writer identified how cultural forces left many women of her era both unhappy, powerless, confused, and clueless.

Women's liberation followed. SOCIAL CONSCIOUSNESS-RAISING became common. Consciousness-raising had already begun in America during the Civil Rights Movement, telling it like it is: *What is happening to make you feel bad? Put words to that. Stop blaming yourself. Identify the problem correctly. Then fix it.*

Historically that process required calling out the unfairness of "Separate but Equal" laws. Also questioning why women earned less than men for doing identical work. Social consciousness-raising was needed before anyone could effectively pursue social activism.

Demanding social change also helped millions of people with their personal development. In ways that hadn't been possible previously, personal identity could be strengthened.

Fact is, you can't claim your rights socially without naming both yourself and whichever lifestyle problem needs to be fixed.

A different sort of consciousness-raising is necessary for Empath Empowerment. The process could be called "SPIRITUAL CONSCIOUSNESS-RAISING." Besides assisting individuals, this helps humanity to evolve spiritually.

Decades ago, in the era of Flower Power, millions of activists led the world in pursuit of social justice. Now our current era invites a new group of leaders to help humanity awaken spiritually.

We're still learning what to call this time of change. Shall we call it "Moving into The Age of Energy"? Life after "The Shift"? Beginning to live in the "Age of Aquarius"? Post-postmodern life in the Third Millennium? I call this new time the "Age of Energy."

Whatever you name it, surely you've noticed. Collectively we are learning new ways to reach out socially. Seems to me, changes in human consciousness are outpacing even the super-fast growth of technology.

These changes are bigger than anything experienced directly by you or me. It may take hundreds of years to fully understand the impact of all these changes. Already I'm certain of one thing. We empaths, as a group, have an important role to play in this spiritual transformation.

Living in this new Age of Energy, the world's empaths are invited to wake up our consciousness and our talent. We're called to make a huge contribution to life on earth. But before we can fulfill this destiny we must learn a complete set of skills to support our gifts.

In retrospect, haven't you been claiming a kind of liberation for yourself? Not some social shift, like the collective awakening of the Civil Rights Movement. More an internal version of waking up.

Come to think of it, wouldn't a more internal kind of awakening be *appropriate* for us as empaths? In essence, the power of an empath is internal, not about obvious objective reality.

Awakening Empath, actualizing this inner potential is required for your fulfillment. Hidden though your empath gifts may be, they define you just as much as skin color or gender identity or how much you're paid at work.

Admittedly, appreciating your empathic nature is trickier, being hidden and internal. Empath gifts show neither in behavior nor facial expression nor anything else in conscious, objective reality. Instead your empath gifts are subjective, energetic, deeply personal, and spiritual in nature.

As you're reading these words, maybe you're remembering what drove you to an empath's version of consciousness-raising. Probably it began with facing some practical problems (like the drip-drip-drip analogy in *The Empowered Empath*).

Did you also notice identity problems? So many empaths have told me stories like this one from Kyle.

Note: Quotations throughout this book come from memory. Anecdotes are true, just not reported verbatim. Also, first names used here are fictitious unless paired with last names. Fair warning: Dialogues in upcoming Q&A Sections will be either reconstructed or fictitious, based on my experience teaching Empath Empowerment®. Okay, back to Kyle's tale.

I told my boss at work how I have been having problems. I'm sensitive in a way that is often overwhelming. This isn't just about being a Highly Sensitive Person, either. It's more than that.

Did my boss understand? Ha! I was told, "Stop complaining. Just turn it off. Hey, that's what I do."

How could Kyle's boss give such unhelpful advice? Quite simple. That person wasn't an empath.

Maybe you have had similar experiences, whether it was your boss at work or your lover; a psychotherapist or a teacher; your brother or sister or co-worker. Kyle had a problem without a name, and others called it a weakness.

Don't blame non-empaths. They can't understand. With all due respect, they lack the capacity to understand, based in personal experience. Besides, empath abilities have not been discussed, in print or elsewhere, until relatively recently.

In *The Empowered Empath* you learned that only 1 in 20 people has been born as an empath. More surprisingly, perhaps, only 1 in 4 Highly Sensitive Persons (HSPs) is an empath. Important though it is to acknowledge an HSP's sensitivity, empath talent is qualitatively different.

You have begun to appreciate that you really do possess special kinds of sensitivity. Moreover, they have shaped your life since birth.

"Just turn it off" cannot work for you because, unlike most other persons — sensitive or not — you have real empath gifts to manage. Knowing this, your sense of self can only grow stronger through naming yourself appropriately as an empath.

Being an empath doesn't make you better than others. However, it does make you decidedly different. Consciousness-raising about those differences? Now that's the start of empowerment.

Owning Your Particular Set of Empath Gifts

Naming yourself as an "Empath" began to align your personal sense of identity. So that really was a good start.

It was only a start, however. Even the naming process needed more development before you could develop effective skills.

Why? By now the word "Empath" is used in pop culture far more widely than 15 years ago. Which is good.

When the first how-to book for empaths was published, it didn't even include that word in the title. (And it wasn't until many years after publication that I had the headslapper thought, "What word is missing in that title, *Empowered by Empathy*"?)

So it helps that today the word "Empath" is used plenty. Unfortunately, "Empath" is often used in ways that are more confusing than helpful. Such as? Defining it as "Someone who feels other people's feelings," or claiming that an empath is somebody who requires psychological boundary work.

In *The Empowered Empath* I sought to remedy confusions like these. You learned accurate names for 15 very different empath gifts. You were coached to discover what is lovely about each one that you possess.

To help you gain skills, these gifts were defined fully, not just the pretty parts. You were alerted to distinctive problems that can accompany each of those empath gifts, at least until solid skills are gained.

Of course, these problems were not put in the context of your personal shortcomings. (For a change?) You were merely informed that each magnificent empath gift has a flip side.

I hope you found it comforting how every born empath with that particular gift has, most likely, suffered from struggles similar to your own. Naming like this helps an empath to sort out past history: *Not your bad! Just a temporary byproduct of your talent when not yet accompanied by skill.*

As an empath coach, I believe that appropriate ownership of empath gifts is tremendously important.

Developing Compassion Along with Your Skill

Awakening Empath, self-compassion may have resulted from Step ONE for becoming a skilled empath. Because empath talent isn't like most other innate talents, waiting in the background until you develop it. All empaths, without exception, are born with their gifts turned ON.

Of course, that has included you. Unskilled empath merges used to happen to you every day.

And each of those countless unskilled merges caused problems: Drip-drip-drip from your empath's faucet.

Your energy field became cluttered with other people's energetic garbage; subconscious junk that was (by definition) hidden from your conscious awareness.

Although that super-quick process of flying in spirit wasn't usually clear to your conscious mind, guess what? Your conscious mind still had to cope with the consequences.

All those stuck energies from random Imported STUFF! And it was so easy to interpret that subconscious clutter as personal weakness.

Awakening Empath, you deserve to feel proud of your empath gifts, every single one. Yet you still might need to grieve a bit over how you used to suffer back in the day, while merely talented and not yet skilled.

Understandably, being unskilled as an empath was deeply confusing. Confusing especially because empath gifts operate differently than other human gifts.

~ For example, suppose that Emmanuel was born with great mathematical ability. Math is done by the conscious mind, in objective reality. Education could help Emmanuel to refine his gift. Over time, he might specialize in probability, statistics, or number theory. What if you asked him as a six-year-old, "What kind of boy are you?" He might have said, "I like to play with numbers."

~ Another example: Audrey was born with superb mechanical intelligence. While a toddler she began taking toys apart, then putting them back together. Consciously she knew just what she was doing; for her, physical objects were delightful mechanical puzzles. What if you asked her, as a six-year-old, "What kind of girl are you?" Audrey might have replied, "I like putting things back together."

Every human alive has multiple gifts. Granted, we don't necessarily have the same ones as Emmanuel or Audrey. Usually, though, our human gifts work on an as-needed basis. Consciously, too.

Mechanical intelligence and math aptitude operate in a manner that is totally different from anything empath. If Audrey's mother told her to stop taking toys apart, the kid could simply stop.

Okay, more likely, she might have pitched a tantrum, then stopped. The point is, Audrey could easily stop if she chose. Her gift involves consciously doing something in objective reality, a relatively easy choice to control.

By contrast, it takes a pretty special parent to fathom the mysteries of empath talent.

In your own childhood, did anyone send you the memo? And how many empaths inspired you by demonstrating Skilled Empath Merge?

During this advanced part of our Program for Empath Empowerment, you will learn an assortment of techniques to safely fly in spirit. Still, that doesn't change your history.

In the past, lack of knowledge denied you the inspiration of Skilled Empath Merge. Or even knowing that you had empath talent. Could be, this aspect of your personal history is pretty sad.

Something great you were born to do... yet you never even knew what it was called? Meanwhile, every day of your life, you were busily engaged in subconscious merges that brought you into the consciousness of random people, animals, plants, whatever.

Earth School for humans is usually based on having one consistent sense of self. Subconsciously life is about "Me me me."

Among people with basic mental health, this holds true for 19 out of 20 people. Well, you are — and always have been — an exception to that majority rule.

Until you read earlier books in this Empath Empowerment series, you had been traveling in consciousness how often? Maybe 1% of your waking hours.

Who knows the exact statistic? That would vary from person to person.

It might depend on the number of empath gifts you have in this lifetime. Furthermore, the percentage might also depend on your degree of talent, overall, as an empath. My hunch is, more talent and more gifts add up to the highest percentage of spontaneous unskilled empath merges.

Eventually scientific research may document all the unskilled merges in the typical day of a young empath. Then we'll know definitively how all those split-split seconds add up.

Meanwhile, don't wait. Consider your sense of self validated. And know that the amount of previous unskilled empath merges you went through was... Plenty, and more than enough to be comfortable!

Having your consciousness identified with the energy field of another person — even if this used to happen to you only 0.0001% of the time — would have been way confusing.

Subconsciously it's challenging enough for adults to deal with their own pain. What happens when this is compounded by directly experiencing pain belonging to other people, and with no way of distinguishing which is which?

Hey, you would know.

By all means, take a few extra moments, as needed, to acknowledge how much you used to suffer as an unskilled empath.

And then let's look forward to your prospects for a greatly improved future. Turning your empath gifts OFF as a matter of habit has made it so much easier for you to think and feel and eat and pray and love... as yourself.

Something even more strengthening for your sense of self happened as a result of Step TWO in our Program for Empath Empowerment. Because that's when you learned essential techniques to keep your empath gifts turned OFF and to vanquish Imported STUFF.

Now Step THREE in this Program for Empath Empowerment will change your life even more.

CHAPTER 2

Basics Required for Skilled Empath Merge

Awakening Empath, you are so very well prepared to do the deepest kind of perception available to humans living now: That would be Skilled Empath Merge.

Here comes a checklist of what is required for safe and productive empath merge. How many of these basics have become routine for you? Let's turn this checklist into a quiz.

Skilled Empath's Quiz. REQUIREMENTS

Which of these do you think is required before you can successfully and safely do Skilled Empath Merge? Answer TRUE or FALSE. Then scroll down for the answers.

1. You have to work at being an empath in the first place. No pain, no gain.   T   F

2. If you want to give to others, you're ready to do Skilled Empath Merge.   T   F

3. If you are curious about others, you're ready to do Skilled Empath Merge.   T   F

4. If you have a great relationship with your guides, and consult them all day long, you're ready to do Skilled Empath Merge.   T   F

5. If you are used to doing energy medicine, like Reiki, you're ready to do Skilled Empath Merge.   T   F

6. If you have great psychological wisdom, you're ready
   to do Skilled Empath Merge.   T   F

7. If it would be too unbearable NOT to do an
   empath merge, you *must* be ready.   T   F

ANSWERS. Requirements

1. You have to work at being an empath in the first place.
No pain, no gain.

FALSE. Either you were born as an empath or you were not. No
work was required to make yourself that.

Granted, meticulous preparation has been part of this Program for
Empath Empowerment. Without practice at keeping your empath
gifts OFF, you would not appreciate the contrast of flying in spirit.

2. If you want to give to others, you're ready to do Skilled
Empath Merge.

FALSE. Doing Skilled Empath Merge does not have to be about
giving to others. That will be your judgment call in that particular
situation.

Usually, Awakening Empath, you will probably not tell other
people what you learn about them. Instead that knowledge will
become your private treasure, a secret source of wisdom. If you
do choose to divulge this, use the separate skill set called "Tact."

For helping others, yes, you can follow up on Skilled Empath Merge
with healing skills from Rosetree Energy Spirituality, like cutting
cords of attachment or replacing outdated, negative thought
forms. Other skill sets can be learned from Energy Medicine or
Energy Psychology or professional training as a psychotherapist.

Besides any of that, you can follow up by using your
skills as a good friend, a loving parent, etc. Otherwise...

How VERY FALSE it would be, assuming that a burning need to give equates with something wonderful to give.

Sure, giving can be noble. Regrettably, it giving can sometimes mask patterns of projecting one's personal needs onto others. Fortunately, a huge protection from doing that has been built into this Program for Empath Empowerment: All that emphasis on first turning your empath gifts OFF.

By strengthening your personal sense of identity, you are more likely to offer others help that is useful. Even for their sake, keep on using your core skills of "Coming Home," "Empath's First Aid," and "I Like."

3. *If you are curious about others, you're ready to do Skilled Empath Merge.*

FALSE. Curiosity is beautiful. Motivating, too, for doing Skilled Empath Merge.

However, excessive curiosity about energies can lead to a floaty life. Especially if you have great curiosity, it is so important to limit your daily minutes of "Technique Time." Twenty minutes total, per day, is plenty for any methods involving energies, self-analysis, meditation, prayer... or other inner activities that take you away from human, objective reality. From now on, I'll be referring to this as OFFICIAL TECHNIQUE TIME.

For your fastest progress as an empath, take no more than 20 minutes of Official Technique Time per day. Total!

4. *If you have a great relationship with your guides, and consult them all day long, you're ready to do Skilled Empath Merge.*

FALSE. Empath skills have nothing to do with psychic development, exploring paranormal experiences, etc. Neither are techniques of Skilled Empath Merge some kind of Astral

Crowd-Sourcing, where the more guides and spirits you get on board, the better.

What if you do have strong psychic interests? Before doing any technique of Skilled Empath Merge, give yourself at least three days without any consultations with angels or guides.

Technically, there are many reasons for this precaution. Most simply, consider it a fast from astral involvement. It will protect you energetically and ground your empath merges into a very human sense of identity.

Meanwhile, your life is about You, The Human, right?

5. *If you are used to doing energy medicine, like Reiki, you're ready to do Skilled Empath Merge.*

FALSE. Techniques of energy medicine can be wonderful, whether Reiki or Eden Energy Medicine or Healing Touch, etc. However, it is very easy for an energy medicine enthusiast to go way over 20 daily minutes of Official Technique Time.

Can you stick to this time limit, even if you do energy medicine professionally? Sure. At the start of your session, take a minute to read your client's energies. Then mechanically use your skills. You don't have to feeeeeeeeeeeeeeeeeel every little thing. Diagnose through noticing energies, then treat. Maybe towards the end of that session you will need one more minute to check on how your client is doing. Two minutes per appointment, that's all.

And yes, Awakening Empath, you can make the distinction between reading energy and mechanically fixing up problems with energy.

Whatever your profession, it's wise to time your explorations of energy. Consider yourself warned. Enthusiasm over energy can run away with your human sense of self.

Although that can happen; it can also be remedied. Just budget your Technique Time wisely.

Every minute of Skilled Empath Merge will count, too. Good old clock time! Don't live like Eve, a talented energy healer who threw her life way out of balance, and why? Because, rather than telling time, she was waiting for what felt like "Enough."

6. *If you have great psychological wisdom, you're ready to do Skilled Empath Merge.*

FALSE. Skilled Empath Merge is a great way to supplement your psychological wisdom. Just make sure you are not trying to substitute anything outside this Program for Empath Empowerment for the prerequisites that have been given so far.

Once I taught a series of two workshops for empaths. It was part of a book tour in Los Angeles, America's capital of Woo-Woo, where many students considered themselves exceptionally advanced, both spiritually and psychologically.

Some of these students insisted on signing up only for Empath Empowerment Part Two. Perhaps it seemed insulting to them, being asked to associate with the mere beginners who were taking Part One.

No insult was intended. Empath Empowerment is a distinctive set of skills. Give yourself (and this full skill set) a chance by making yourself ready. Feeling ready because you know you are wise? With all respect, that might not be relevant.

7. *If it would be too unbearable NOT to do an empath merge, you must be ready to do Skilled Empath Merge.*

FALSE. Sweet but FALSE.

Granted, many other things in life do work that way. For instance, a couple is wondering whether they need to wait before having a child. And even though common sense tells them to delay, that waiting feels just unbearable. Then might be a good time to take a leap of faith and start making that baby.

I'm not an expert on all the life situations where feeling a push from within equates to God's voice in human form.

When it comes to training empaths, however, I have learned some things the hard way. That includes saying "Wait" to my passionately motivated, eager students who felt they deserved a shortcut. There is no substitute for the habit of living with empath gifts OFF.

The True Requirements for Safe, Skilled Empath Merge

Requirements for responsibly doing Skilled Empath Merge are not about your degree of longing. Responsible requirements are quite straightforward:

1. You have learned to own and *embrace your empath gifts,* using the information provided in *The Empowered Empath* — or equivalent depth knowledge. What if you do not feel a "Stand up in church and testify" degree of certainty? No problem. You are hereby authorized to stop holding your breath over this topic and start trusting yourself.

2. You are committed to *turning your empath gifts OFF.* This has become part of your regular routine. For at least a couple of weeks now, you have done that reasonably well. (The occasional slip-up is no big deal. Learning means learning.)

3. In your lifestyle, you have given yourself *at least a week* with a maximum of 20 daily minutes of Official Technique Time.

4. You have *explored each technique and workaround so far* in this Program for Empath Empowerment. Not that you must feel ready to crown yourself as Supreme Emperor of Perfection at Doing Every Technique. Nope, simply exploring like a good sport, maybe even muddling your way through. But game.

Missing any of those four requirements? Please, go back and complete them. Your empath gifts will be waiting for you, magnificent resources for the huge fun called "Skilled Empath Merge." Well, now that you *are* ready, let's move forward to something vital.

A Golden Preparation Process

Why do I call this preparation process "Golden"?

Because of attributes like "Valuable" and "Doesn't require polishing." This golden sequence of specific techniques will position your awareness best for Skilled Empath Merge. Simultaneously, the sequence will protect your energies.

By now, you already know most of these techniques. Well, here comes the full sequence.

1. Choose the particular technique you will use. (Okay, that part hasn't come yet, but soon.)

2. Prepare the environment accordingly. This means:

⁓ Do your reasonable best to prevent interruptions. Turn off all electronic gizmos that might ring or vibrate or otherwise jerk your consciousness back into physical reality. Remove cigarettes, chewing gum, food from mouth. (Yes, even chocolate.)

⁓ Gather pen and paper for quick scribble notes. If alone, you can substitute your favorite electronic recording device, into which you will speak your findings out loud.

⁓ Choose the individual you will research. (Details about this will depend on the technique being pursued, so more on this topic will be forthcoming.)

⁓ Sit comfortably. Head not supported. Legs and arms free, rather than crossed. (Provides a smoother energy flow while doing the Skilled Empath Merge.)

3. Read over the technique instructions. Not doing, simply previewing. Place those instructions where you can easily peek at them while you go through technique steps.
4. Get Big. Hey, you know this technique by now!
5. Set an Intention. Coming up soon!
6. Take Vibe-Raising Breaths as appropriate. Specifics about fancy breathing will be explained as needed for the particular technique for Skilled Empath Merge.

And there you go. Are you excited? This teacher of yours is thrilled! Proud of you, too. By now you have learned invaluable habits that will stand you in good stead for becoming a Master Empath:

- Allowing — valuing your experience, whatever happens while doing the steps of a technique.
- Scribble writing — a quick-and-sloppy way to record highlights from a technique.
- Energy hygiene — staying in a technique until it is officially over. And then...
- Officially ending the technique when it's done.
- Grounding Breaths, to be used as appropriate.

You see, Awakening Empath, each technique you learn for Skilled Empath Merge will begin with an identical preparation process. Next comes the main, exciting, distinctive part of a technique. Following that, your technique will officially end.

After which time, please:

Go back to being yourself. That's your regular, workable sense of self.

Go back to living with empath gifts turned OFF, as usual. Yes, your new usual as a well-adjusted human!

So let's get going, gathering momentum as you pursue this Program for Empath Empowerment.

CHAPTER 3

How to Start Every Skilled Empath Merge

Awakening Empath, each time you do Skilled Empath Merge, you will follow the same sequence. It's as straightforward as counting from 1 to 7.

Your self-authority can remain constant through that entire sequence. How? Through your sense of Me-Me-Me-Me-Me:

I like. I decide.

I am willing to be spontaneous.

Forget about doing a perfect job; instead I'll just go step-by-step.

I can do this. And I'm curious what I will find.

1. Choose Your Discovery Person

Each Empath Merge will be inform you about a particular person, your Discovery Person. Make that a *human* person, at least for your first three times doing any new technique in our Program for Empath Empowerment.

Also make that a sober person. By which I don't mean mood but substances. Just as you would never do Skilled Empath Merge while under the influence, it is deeply unhelpful to merge your consciousness with someone who is tipsy, whether pleasantly buzzed or high as a kite.

Not only could this lead to confusing experiences during the empath merge itself. You would put yourself at risk for cluttering up your aura with astral debris like stuck spirits who are often involved in chemical highs. (To learn more about this type of STUFF, see *Use Your Power of Command for Spiritual Cleansing and Protection.*)

By now, you can actually choose for yourself when you will do an empath merge with somebody. This discernment and freedom will make your life so much easier in the long run. Do you realize what a safeguard it can be, making a conscious choice?

As a skilled empath, you always get to choose your Discovery Person. Back in the day, most of your empath merges were random; usually you didn't even know you were doing them. Now you totally get to choose.

For our first techniques of Skilled Empath Merge, please choose a real, live person right there with you in the room. Later you will learn techniques for Skilled Empath Merge that you can do incognito and even remotely. Awakening Empath, you may love that freedom as much I do!

In person or at a distance, you alone will get to choose. That is one delightful aspect of your self-authority. Who decides which Discovery Person? Me-Me-Me-Me-Me.

2. Choose Your Technique

This Program for Empath Empowerment presents you with a systematically arranged sequence of techniques for Skilled Empath Merge. We'll start with the easiest first.

Easiest for most people, anyway. Certain techniques are bound to become your personal favorites, and neither you nor I can tell in advance which ones they will be.

Long term, all you will really need is one empath merge technique that you like for in-person. Plus one technique that you like for doing Skilled Empath Merge with a photo.

Just for fun, the first technique I teach you will be my personal favorite for in-person Skilled Empath Merge.

While first going through this array of techniques, I recommend that you follow the sequence as it is presented. Awakening Empath, it would be wise to experiment with each of these techniques for two or three times, at a minimum. Practice even more if you wish to adapt that technique to use with a non-human Discovery Person.

What if, for instance, you are really excited about doing Skilled Empath Merge with your dog, Rover? Then explore each new technique three times with some human volunteers, either the same Discovery Person on three different days or three different volunteers one after another. Afterwards, if you have Animal Empath Talent, sure. Go ahead and experiment, doing Skilled Empath Merge with Rover as your Discovery Person.

For a technique that requires consent, like "I Want to Hold Your Hand," you cannot control whether your Discovery Person will agree and cooperate, Rover included. At least you always get to choose which Discovery Person to invite.

3. Choose an Appropriate Time

Awakening Empath, that means an appropriate time for yourself.

Choose a time when you feel clear and awake, not drowsy. Skilled Empath Merge is not passive, like binge watching your fourth episode-in-a-row from a favorite series at 2:00 a.m.

Also important? Never do a technique for Skilled Empath Merge while drunk or stoned on recreational chemicals. Or even when angry.

You know those moments after a big fight when you feel oh-so-inspired? (It seems.) Right then, you may feel driven to share the perfect insult or insight. It feels like, right this minute, you absolutely must tell that horrible person... whatever. There can be an almost physical urge to grab your phone right now and scream out those words.

Well, how effective would that really be as a way to fix your relationship? Oboy, I hope you never find out from personal experience. If it can help, let me share my experience with this sort of thing: Not good.

Definitely, avoid attempting any Skilled Empath Merge when you're on the attack and seeking an extra emotional weapon.

On a happier theme, what if you are in the perfect mood for Skilled Empath Merge? Let's say that you're feeling great. A large number of Discovery People might be available, too.

Well, pace yourself. Bigger results will come from daily practice for 10 minutes a day than from longer practices.

Any day at all, remember to stick to your 20 daily minutes of Official Technique Time. You're into this empath lifestyle for a major marathon, not some big, dramatic sprint.

Choosing an appropriate time, staying in charge of your schedule, is such a great way to honor Me-Me-Me-Me-Me.

4. Create an Ideal-Ish Environment

Skilled Empath Merge does not require concentration. You will not be forcing in any way. You will, however, be paying attention gently (which is the most effective way to notice subtle experiences). For this a relatively quiet environment would be preferable.

Select a non-chaotic place, too. Prevent interruptions from roommates, etc. This will protect you from doing the inner equivalent of this: Speeding down the highway of consciousness, then slamming on the brakes.

Likewise multi-tasking is completely inappropriate. Even chewing gum would be too great a distraction. Turn those electronic "essentials" off completely, avoiding all calls, set-on-vibrates, texts, and tweets.

Such demands on your attention would take it shallow, complicated, and wide. Whereas Skilled Empath Merge is designed to take you simple and deep.

Pets in the room or small children? Anybody other than your Discovery Person? Please avoid that distraction. Even when very, very skilled at empath merge, you will do your best in an environment that honors Me-Me-Me-Me-Me... and the specialness of what is being done.

5. Technology Chosen by Me-Me-Me-Me-Me

Recording equipment has always been recommended for doing techniques of Skilled Empath Merge. Living now, of course, we can show our style by the technology we select.

Maybe you adore the ease of pen and paper. Alternatively you might prefer a tablet, a laptop, a digital recorder, or technology that didn't exist yet when I published this book.

Just make sure that your choice is effort-free. Save learning the latest technology for a different occasion. For best results, make your chosen technology an easy extension of Me-Me-Me-Me-Me.

6. A Preparation Process Starring Guess Who?

That Preparation Process you have learned is so very useful, it will be tucked into every single Skilled Empath Merge technique in this Program for Empath Empowerment.

One caution for those of you who are not big fans of following routines. Make an exception for the routine Preparation Process in Skilled Empath Merge. This is essential, not optional.

Consider it like tuning your guitar strings before you start to play.

Hey, if you're all alone with this book, you may be tempted to entertain ideas like these: *"I've done it once. I understand the concept. I don't have time. I'm too smart. I'm too special. The number of breaths in my Life Contract is being used up waaaaay too fast. How tragic it would be if I had to plod through three entire minutes because of doing my Preparation Process!"*

Well, don't go there, Awakening Empath. This Preparation Process will position your consciousness appropriately. Besides, with practice, it really will take three minutes or less.

Consciousness preparation is a very efficient way to awaken the depths of Me-Me-Me-Me-Me.

7. Return to Me-Style Reality with Energy Hygiene

Preparation Process will be followed by your experience with the specifics of doing Skilled Empath Merge, plus afterwards you may spend some time communicating with your Discovery Person. When doing a remote technique, an advanced form of Skilled Empath Merge, you might journal a bit, making a quick log about your progress.

None of this afterwards time need count as Official Technique Time, as it lies in the realm of surface human reality.

However after you finish any technique for empath merge, be sure to use good clear labelling to yourself. Know when you start a technique. Know when you end it.

ENERGY HYGIENE is my name for that simple use of free will. Do you have a dog that you love? You still won't drink out of his water dish, will you? That's regular hygiene. The consciousness kind has you separate human awareness from puppy. I mean, from noticing energy.

Energy hygiene is indispensable for maintaining a strong, human sense of identity. Thinking something like "Technique over" is vital for energy hygiene. So many benefits can flow from taking that simple thought before opening your eyes and returning to regular reality. "Technique over" means:

- Back to human. Your kind of human.
- Back to normal positioning of consciousness in surface-level subjective reality, regular thinking and feeling.
- Back to interacting with physical things, moving your body, using your senses. (Extra benefit? Dealing with objective reality can help your consciousness to feel free and clean.)
- Back, in short, to Me-Me-Me-Me-Me in everyday life.

Actively do a technique or not. Either-or. To become a Master Empath, you need to honor this difference. Your healthy sense of identity depends on it.

Speaking of Healthy

Skilled Empath Merges are subtle, done with awareness. Yet they are also potentially startling, surprising, and can be way more intense than those unskilled empath merges you used to do.

You know how, with hypnosis-inducing recordings, there will be cautions like, "Do not do this while operating heavy machinery"?

The same goes for the consciousness-shifting techniques of Skilled Empath Merge. Never do any technique for Skilled Empath Merge while operating machinery, driving a car, cooking with a stove, even walking with scissors.

Before doing any of those things after Skilled Empath Merge, give yourself a good 30 minutes of transition time. Just to be on the safe side. Protecting the Awakening Empath.

CHAPTER 4

Prepare Your Discovery Person (and Yourself)

Skilled Empath Merge with a real-time, live person is the biggest fun of all. Experiences will be most vivid when your Discovery Person stands right in the room with you, eager for you to fly in spirit and report back.

At least that in-person vividness has been true for me, doing many thousands of Skilled Empath Merges. The joy and freshness are definitely stronger in person.

What if, in the future, you wind up doing empath merges as part of your professional work?

By then you have no doubts about the accuracy and helpfulness. Even so, you may always prefer in-person experiences.

What if it won't be convenient for you to find a willing human subject?

Really? Are you sure?

Then skip ahead to "Find Your Truth Sight Research Tool" in Chapter 8. Otherwise, why not start with the easiest and best?

Skilled Empath's Quiz.
YOUR "CHOOSE WISELY" CHECKLIST

Some potential candidates for an empath merge will be a delight. Others would be a drag. Avoid them.

How to tell the difference? Develop EMPATH STREET SMARTS, sensible ways to protect yourself while doing Skilled Empath Merge.

The following quiz can help. Go through this simple checklist, where I will use Wyatt as a possible Discovery Person.

Answer **TRUE** or **FALSE**.

1. Is Wyatt physically here with me in the room?   T   F

2. Will Wyatt feel comfortable, going into a separate room with me one-on-one, while we do this empath technique?   T   F

3. Regarding substances, right now, am I reasonably certain that Wyatt is not drunk or stoned?   T   F

4. And can he bear to spend the next few minutes without smoking a cigarette, chewing tobacco, chewing gum, eating, or drinking?   T   F

5. Is Wyatt someone I know well enough personally to offer this treat, a Skilled Empath Merge?   T   F

6. Since I know Wyatt that well, I will have a general sense of him before asking. Might he say "Yes" to my invitation?   T   F

7. Based on what I know of him so far, would Wyatt say "Yes" because he is at least a little bit curious about this process or what I might tell him?   T   F

8. Is it likely that Wyatt will either refuse my invitation or scoff at whatever I tell him?   T   F

9. In case it takes me an extra-long time, being a beginner, does Wyatt have 15 minutes for hanging out with me for this Skilled Empath Merge?   T   F

10. Does Wyatt possess enough maturity to be quiet while I am doing a technique that demands my inner silence?   T   F

11. Might Wyatt actually listen politely to what I tell him after I do this Skilled Empath Merge?   T   F

ANSWERS. Your "Choose Wisely" Checklist

TRUE answers are required for every question, except for trick Question #7. A good choice of Discovery Person will score perfectly before being invited to the treat of your Skilled Empath Merge. What you are asking is not too much, not for a certain kind of person.

Don't be afraid to use this quiz on every possible Discovery Person. It does not make you excessively demanding. You're protecting yourself, making a long-term investment in your talent and developing skill.

Acknowledge to yourself: Wyatt might flunk this test despite being a wonderful friend, a great lover, a fine neighbor, an adorable daughter or whatever. (Sure, this "Wyatt" could be female. Why not?)

How about requiring that your Discovery Person be strongly interested in this empath aspect of your life? This is not required, any more than Wyatt needs to care particularly about empaths to qualify as a wonderful friend, a great lover, a fine neighbor, an adorable daughter, a superb professional athlete, an upstanding member of your church, exceptionally talented as a dental hygienist, etc.

Awakening Empath, part of your preparation for Skilled Empath Merge has been your shift into a strong, balanced human identity. By now, you have a firm hold on objective reality. Well, combine that longstanding common sense with your new Empath Street Smarts. Don't risk your credibility with a work colleague or a first date by introducing the topic of Skilled Empath Merge.

Don't risk your self-respect, either. Any prospective Discovery Person will receive a treat in return for volunteering. It's not like you will just be receiving a huge favor because Wyatt nobly agrees to be your practice person. You will be doing a favor for Wyatt, providing a Skilled Empath Merge. Do remember that you are giving more than you're getting. Invite somebody who might appreciate that.

Pop the Question

How complicated does it have to be, inviting your discovery person to receive a Skilled Empath Merge?

Asking is simple, once you have privately done the basic quiz. Explain just enough. You can always answer questions later. For example, you might say:

Wyatt, I have been learning how to do a kind of depth personality profiling called "Skilled Empath Merge." I would like to do this for you, just for fun. Altogether it will take approximately 10 minutes. Are you interested?

Once you have the go ahead, prepare in the practical ways that follow.

Logistics for Your Empath Research

At the end of a Skilled Empath Merge with a consenting Discovery Person, you will share *some* of what you learned. That said, you would be wise to make notes on *all* that you learn. It is good practice to make notes every single time that you purposely fly in spirit. Get pen and paper handy, or choose another recording device that is voiceless.

Take your Discovery Person to the room where you will be doing this empath merge (if this location is different from where your invitation was just accepted).

Go through your familiar routine of preventing distractions, such as telling others that the two of you will be back soon; turning off your phone and asking your Discovery Person to do the same.

Keep instructions for doing your technique within easy view. No need to feel self-conscious about using this teaching tool. Only practice will familiarize you with the steps.

Now is the time to prepare your partner for this exercise. After your Discovery Person has given permission, a bit more preparation is needed. It's called communication, folks. Begin once you are in the space where research will take place.

Summarize what to expect:

I will be doing a technique for Skilled Empath Merge. Before we get started, let's practice how I will hold your hand for part of the technique.

When I start my research process, that will be in silence. Briefly I will hold your hand, then let go. You will see me making some notes. When I have finished, I'll announce that I'm back.

Then we can talk, and I will share my discoveries with you. Please don't talk to me until I start talking to you.

Now let's practice the position for my holding your hand as part of the research.

Practice the Physical Position for a Technique of Skilled Empath Merge

Teaching workshops for empaths, I have discovered the funniest thing. Being physically comfortable can make a very big difference for the quality of your experience.

Awakening Empath, either choose comfort or you can jam your body into an awkward position, crossing your ankles, or otherwise making things physically unnecessarily complicated. Please don't. Choose ease and flow and grace, even on a physical level.

Why not skip practicing? Isn't the meaning obvious enough when you read about a physical position, such as "Hold your partner's hand in handshake position"?

Actually, your physical bodies needs to practice the physical position. Remember, your conscious brain isn't all you will need when flying in spirit. So do yourself a favor, Awakening Empath. Take the time required here on Planet Earth to practice a physical skill.

What if you were to follow me around at workshops for empaths? You might laugh to see how many of my brainy, magnificent students perform during their first position practice. They can get themselves into the most contorted, awkward positions. Quickly this is corrected, once I coach them just a bit.

Can you do that fine-tuning without my being physically present? This is a do-it-yourself Program for Empath Empowerment! Just read and take the time to follow the instructions given.

In theory, Skilled Empath Merge may seem mystical or glamorous. Nonetheless, each technique will require practicing a physical position for yourself and/or your Discovery Person. My advice? Start developing good habits now for powerful, purposeful flying in spirit. Always practice the physical position required for a technique.

So practice simple handshake position, with no shaking part to follow. It's a way of holding hands briefly, palms making contact.

Once your practice is done, let go your hands. You'll be ready to start exploring your shiny, new technique.

For this empath, even after so many thousands of explorations, every fresh time that I do a technique for Skilled Empath Merge, it really is shiny and new. Awakening Empath, I wish you that same deliciousness. Practice the technical aspects to ensure smooth, productive techniquing.

Q&A. Practice the Physical Position
for a Technique of Skilled Empath Merge

Q. *What if I feel weirdly self-conscious about practicing a basic handshake, of all things?*

A. Good for you, going step by step, whether you feel weird or not! What does it mean, to have a successful experience? You don't have to feel lovely in every way. Just go through one step at a time.

Skilled Empath Merge isn't some vague, wishey-hopey, feel-good activity. Each technique in this Program for Empath Empowerment is designed to bring you results, that's all. The technique will contain certain steps. Regardless of mood, you do them. Then you get the results, own the skill.

Q. *Why would I need to practice a handshake, for crying out loud? My Discovery Person won't come from Mars, I promise.*

A. Any physical position being used for Skilled Empath Merge should be practiced in advance. While in the regular waking state of consciousness, we are used to making adjustments to physical position. Otherwise we ignore what does not work quite right.

Think about it. Haven't you sometimes shaken hands with a person who missed your palm entirely? What if you reach over and, when connecting, your arm is at an odd angle, a bit uncomfortable?

Then you'll shrug off any awkwardness, right? In everyday life you have conscious attention to spare, with awareness busily computing many variables right on the surface of reality. If something's a significant problem, you solve it.

Now, fast-forward to while you are doing a technique for Skilled Empath Merge. Your physical positioning becomes a launch site for consciousness to fly in spirit — almost like moving into a yoga asana, where the purpose of the physical position is to reposition your awareness. Physically it matters that you get the form correctly.

For our upcoming technique, "I Want to Hold Your Hand," a normal-looking handshake serves a different purpose from any simple, everyday handshake. Ordinarily folks do hit-or-miss variations, oblivious to maximum ease and flow and grace. For techniquing, this handshake position needs to become an effortless physical basis for travel in consciousness.

Prepare now. Then, in technique, you'll get it right.

Q. *What if my practice handshake doesn't seem friendly enough? This handshake won't be accompanied by smiling at my partner or even looking at her. Won't she notice how this behavior isn't normal?*

A. Maybe. Which wouldn't be a bad thing, necessarily. Without making a big deal of it, you are educating each Discovery Person with whom you do this technique. Wordlessly, you're conveying a message: "This is something special, a Skilled Empath Merge. It is worth our taking a moment to prepare. I am using a specialized skill to reposition my consciousness."

In today's world, space is not the final frontier. Consciousness is the final frontier.

Both you and your Discovery Person may be new to the research into consciousness called "Skilled Empath Merge."

For you, this will be way different from old ways that you used to slip-slide into another person's subconscious experience, with zero energy hygiene. Now you are purposely taking a bit of time, preparing for experience that can be way clearer. Plus your energy field will stay bright, uncluttered by Imported STUFF.

As for doing this particular Skilled Empath Merge, a bit of official physical practice can help you significantly. Thanks to your dress rehearsal, that empath's handshake position will be done rapidly, physically spot-on, and comfortably. All of which will make it easier for you to transcend the environment entirely, quietly blasting off into your altered state of consciousness.

Afterwards you will share your findings, giving a special treat to your Discovery Person. So what if you're taking a moment now to prepare? That can add to the sense of specialness.

Q. *What if my Discovery Person wants to play along with me? Can I just show her my instructions, or coach her?*

A. Sorry, but doing either one of these would be highly irresponsible. In this Age of Energy, many people are playing with consciousness as though it were one more cute, disposable new toy. Not so.

Give yourself credit. In advance of doing this technique, you prepared yourself thoroughly. You made sure that this Skilled Empath Merge would add to your sense of identity, not confuse you. Don't disrespect your own efforts by compromising the integrity of this Program for Empath Empowerment. Whether your Discovery Person is joking or serious, please join me in upholding standards.

Lend her your copy of *The Empowered Empath*. Even better, encourage her to buy her own copy, because that will demonstrate more of a commitment from her side.

Q. *What if she thinks I'm being a showoff? Or a snob!*

A. Show your friend that you take your identity as an empath seriously. Empath skills can be real — for you they are that already. And she can get those skills too, only not as a casual game.

On behalf of the world's growing community of skilled empaths, avoid compromising a technique that is potentially life-changing. Never play with techniques in this Program for Empath Empowerment, trying to turn them into a few tweets or tips, like some form of trivial pursuit.

Incidentally, your Discovery Person may be impressed by your politely saying no. Demonstrating that you have standards can add power to your role as a skilled empath.

Q. *What if my Discovery Person has been involved in this Program for Empath Empowerment. Do we have to take turns doing the technique or could we do it simultaneously?*

A. Either way would work fine. Choose whichever sequence you prefer.

CHAPTER 5

Tact

When doing any Skilled Empath Merge in person, record whatever you find during the technique. Record it all. But don't necessarily tell it all.

That might be neither kind nor helpful. Here is how to do better:

- ⤳ Record findings for your private educational process.
- ⤳ Share out loud appropriately, as a tactful empath.

Get in the habit of writing down everything, absolutely everything, you experience during a Skilled Empath Merge. Even if writing all this down seems weird to you.

Some of what you write will be Before-and-After. This keeps your conscious and subconscious mind trained on the truth, which is that you are the instrument.

This truth cannot be acknowledged too often. You are the one flying in spirit. Me-Me-Me-Me-Me.

You have your own feelings, thoughts, understandings, physical reactions to life; your own needs, wants; your distinctive sense of humor.

Empath merge provides contrast, made all the more vivid because you have paused long enough on either side of the merge to establish that contrast.

Telling this contrasting part to your Discovery Person would provide too much information. Whereas writing it down for yourself? Brilliant!

Your emerging habit of record-it-all can help you to count everything that happens while you're in technique, in contrast to editing what seems important *while* immersed in the experience.

Besides, some record-it-all can have a side benefit for your personal growth: Maintaining your strong sense of identity. Imagine being interested in yourself as a person! Every day! No matter what!

Already you have come so far at strengthening that sense of identity, Awakening Empath. By noting every single thing, every single time that you do an empath merge, what happens? You remind yourself that this is your process — your doing the technique, your supplement to the routine business of Me-Me-Me-Me-Me.

In Praise of Scribble-Writing

Speaking of your effectiveness at doing a Skilled Empath Merge and, eventually, tact... recorded data serves a very practical purpose.

The notes you make about the travel part of an empathic technique, all this will be about your Discovery Person. Every single bit needs to be written down, uncensored.

Allow this scribble writing to become a spontaneous form of expression, recorded as fast as you can. Trust that putting subtle perception into language is a cumulative skill. Soon you will speak "Empath" fluently.

Awakening Empath, soon you will move deftly in awareness from deep astral and subconscious perceptions... right up to the surface of conscious reality. All this flow of consciousness develops from the relatively simple task of physically recording some words.

Adeptness as a communicator, yes! This is so important, it can move you forward in general on your path of personal development.

So let's celebrate that scribble writing. Do not ever skip this step. It's so quick to do, and will become even quicker for you over time. What else is great about scribble writing? Nothing needs to be tactful... yet.

Isn't one definition of tact "Deciding what to tell and what not to tell"? Tact does not have to mean "Lying." Instead tact is a way to help others through selectively sharing what is appropriate.

Share So You Can Help Your Discovery Person

Doing a technique for Skilled Empath Merge like "I Want to Hold Your Hand," you can receive so much, both the growth process for yourself (cumulative, no matter what) plus a here-and-now, unique experience of researching your partner.

After you have returned from flying in spirit, how are you going to reward the person who helped you?

In the future, reward won't be needed for most empath merge techniques. Because you will do them anonymously, using techniques for secret empath explorations to be learned later in this Program for Empath Empowerment. Direct reward is only required, as a courtesy, during here-and-now interaction with a consenting Discovery Person. When giving back is only fair.

So do it right. Speaking tactfully as an empath? This is an art.

Words that you tell your Discovery Person can validate and inspire. I recommend using the following sequence for reporting on Skilled Empath Merge. I'll even provide some sample language that you can adapt as you see fit.

1. Introduce Perspective

Before you share a single thing about the Skilled Empath Merge, remind your Discovery Person to use self-authority.

Your Discovery Person might want to give this away to any random aura reader or empath. A quick reminder about self-authority can prevent that.

Others who agree to play Discovery Person are skeptical. By acknowledging their self-authority, you demonstrate that you're not trying to lord it over them — which can serve to disarm many a skeptic before you share a single detail.

Thanks for helping me to do this technique for Skilled Empath Merge. Now I can tell you what I learned. Run this by your own sense of what brightens you up (or rings true or feels right). What matters to me is that you keep only whatever you consider helpful.

2. Share Information about the Discovery Person, Not Yourself

As an evolving empath, your personal process is ever-fascinating. To you. But leave aside that part of what you recorded during the scribble writing. (Perhaps think about it later.) Which is the part to tell? Only mention what is relevant and potentially helpful to your Discovery Person.

Some empath gifts involve intuition, or having the distinct sense that you are receiving information about the other person, not yourself.

By contrast, other empath gifts involve oneness, or experiencing within yourself in a way that is really about your Discovery Person.

As you know, still other empath gifts can combine experiences of intuition and oneness.

When sharing your experiences, it isn't horribly wrong to compare the Discovery Person to yourself, but always emphasize that other person. If you do compare your partner to yourself, do this to make your words relatable, positive. There is an art to sharing without offering up too much information.

Just don't chat in the style of a reality show where over-sharing is encouraged and drama desirable. Say only what seems helpful, for example:

Emotionally, you are very different from me. You have more struc-tured feelings, and it's normal for you to keep them a part of your life, rather than take you over.

I also noticed, you have such a strong awareness of being physical. There's a degree of comfort about being in your body, plus a very masculine kind of sensuality.

The way your mind works is very deliberate, like a systematic process of thinking. No, everybody does not think that way! It's wonderful.

I was also impressed by how you connect to the Divine. Seemed to me, you have such a deep sense of devotion, a magnificent spiritual generosity.

3. Start and End with Something Positive

Actually you might choose to make your shared remarks entirely positive. Really that depends on the context for your Skilled Empath Merge.

- ⤳ Just doing a brief exploration with a friend? Personally, I would keep that all positive.

- ⤳ Doing a Skilled Empath Merge with a relative stranger or new acquaintance? Definitely, I would keep that all positive.

What about using your empath skills in conjunction with professional work? After you are experienced with Skilled Empath Merge, you might wish to add this to your relevant professional skill sets. For instance, what if you are a chiropractor, a hypnotist, an acupuncturist, a life coach, a psychotherapist, a Reiki healer?

- ⤳ Then you might take a couple of minutes of Technique Time at the start of your session with the client. You would explain enough so that your client knows what on earth is happening. Then it could be appropriate to describe problems... provided that you will be addressing them during that particular session.

- ⤳ Or you might note those problems and talk about them only at the end of the session, having done a second round of Skilled Empath Merge.

～◦ What about other problems that you will not be able to address during that session? The ethical thing to do is to keep those problems entirely to yourself.

Until you start doing Skilled Empath Merge, you may have no idea how difficult life can be for other people. What if it seems like your Discovery Person, Wyatt, is a mess?

Remember, Wyatt is used to living with that mess. Don't convey alarm. What about the difficulty of finding something positive in all that mess? Keep investigating until you can find something positive. You always can.

Q&A. Sharing in Order to Help Your Discovery Person

Note: The following sequence of questions and answers is based on questioners who have already done some Skilled Empath Merges, anticipating what could come up later.

Q. *I did three merges in a row, once with each of my roommates. After the first merge, I was surprised. After the second, I was absolutely amazed because it was so different. After the third empath merge, I felt high as a kite. How can I even begin to find words for how amazing it is to do a Skilled Empath Merge?*

A. You'll get used to it. Just say something to your Discovery Person, even if it isn't perfect. Languaging is a cumulative skill. Plus it is nice to give back.

Q. *Doing one empath merge was plenty for me, so far. Giving feedback afterwards, I kept saying things like "I don't know" and "I'm not sure." This creeped me out. Probably it did not inspire a whole lot of confidence in me, but I couldn't help it. Did I do the wrong thing, being honest?*

A. Expressing your insecurities about doing something new — that isn't "Being honest." It belongs in the category of TMI (too much information).

Be nice to yourself as you learn something new. Beginners don't feel as secure as they will feel later on. To grow fastest, avoid expressing sentiments like "I'm not sure." Share boldly. You are aiming to help or inspire your Discovery Person. That's the point.

Besides practice, what else can help you to develop more confidence? Remember how every Skilled Empath Merge has an official intention? Sounds as though, before, you might have accidentally slipped into one of those not-so-desirable intentions, like proving something to yourself.

Next time, be sure to choose a worthy intention, like "I am ready to be of service to this person."

Q. *I noticed that Vince, my Discovery Person, is pre-diabetic. What would have been the tactful way to tell him?*

A. There is no tactful way to convey this information. Are you a physician who just gave Vince a lab test?

Q. *No, I just have Medical Empath Talent.*

A. If you already have a professional skill set around helping people with physical healing, then include your findings as part of an appointment for healing.

It is very important that you avoid giving people gratuitous health information. Clearly you mean well. Could be, the information you just experienced is 100% accurate. Even so, unless you are working in a professional setting, it would be inappropriate to share your experiences as an empath.

The skill set from your training as a health professional would include what to say, how to say it, and how to handle problems.

Q. *But Vince is a really good friend. Don't you think it would be right to warn him in any way?*

A. At most, you might suggest that he get a checkup. Leave announcements about the specifics to the doctor who interprets Vince's lab work.

Q. *I feel so sorry for my Discovery Person. I never realized before that my friend Yvonne was so neurotic. I'm pretty sure she is obsessive-compulsive. What is the nice way to break the news to her?*

A. Not.

See the previous round of questions. Transfer the context to psychological healing and being a mental health professional, rather than being a physical healer. The sort of announcement you contemplate would be neither tactful nor ethical nor appropriate. Do not turn Yvonne's casual experience of receiving a brief empath merge into Official Diagnosis Announcement Time.

Q. *But if I told her, maybe she could get medication or something. Yvonne is suffering. Don't I have a moral obligation to help her?*

A. No matter how great your empath skills, they cannot substitute for other skill sets. Today self-taught "experts" aplenty are diagnosing themselves and others through the Internet.

Some of my empath students are mental health professionals. They have told me that this does more harm than good. I believe them. Definitely do not throw around alarming labels like "obsessive-compulsive." At most you might say something like, "Wow, there is so much emotional intensity to being you right now. How do you handle it?"

Q. *Because I am so talented as an empath, I got lots of hits immediately, even while doing the practice position. I couldn't help myself, so I just blurted it out to my friend Connor. I figured that way it wouldn't get in the way of my official empath merge. Do you recommend that, in the future, I should share information like this before or after? Which would be better?*

A. Nice catch, how you noticed that you were not yet doing a Skilled Empath Merge. Getting hits is more related to psychic development. If you are doing psychic work, use your skills (and tact, and ethics) for that work. Keep all this totally separate from doing empath merges.

Reflect for a moment on what you were doing this time with Connor. You were practicing the position for a technique of Skilled Empath Merge. Meanwhile you kept yourself available for intuitive hits. In future, do not mix up these entirely different ways to position your consciousness.

Q. *You don't seem to understand. I am a psychic empath. I am constantly getting messages. Don't I have an obligation to tell my Discovery Person about the wonderful woman who is coming into his life?*

A. Sadly, the term "Psychic empath" confuses many people. And you might be one of them. When teachers of psychic development use this term, know the context. You are receiving instruction in psychic development, not empath skills.

In this Program for Empath Empowerment, there is no such thing as a "psychic empath." Instead you might have many gifts as an empath, all of which you can develop for helping others and improving your own stability as a person. Before doing any more experiments with empath merges, please protect yourself by turning to *The Empowered Empath*.

Go back and do, or re-do, Parts One and Two of becoming a skilled empath. Otherwise you can experience energetic confusions. Inadvertently you may often deposit Imported STUFF in your aura. Problems like these are way more serious than the small inconvenience you asked about in your question about your friend Connor.

Thank you for asking. A teacher like me cannot help unless a student like you asks the relevant questions.

Q. *My Discovery Person insisted on giving me feedback after every sentence. Maria made me feel like it was a quiz and she was going to flunk me. What can I say to keep people from turning this into some kind of guessing game?*

A. Train your Discovery Person. Probably Maria has no idea how to respond to a Skilled Empath Merge. Could be, you prepared her fine initially; then you left blank any training about what to say in response to your telling her about the empath merge.

Continue her education, as needed. For someone like Maria, you could say one of the following, depending on what seems appropriate to the situation.

> ∼ *"Maria, this must be the first time someone gave you a Skilled Empath Merge. Just so you know, this isn't a psychic reading. It isn't about accuracy. I was exploring what it was like for me to experience what it is like to be you. I have been describing some of the things I found that make you special. Feedback isn't required here for my benefit, but if you wish to give some anyway, please wait until the end, ok?"*

> ∼ *"I'm glad you could relate to x, y, and z. Keep that part, Maria. The rest doesn't matter. Remember what I said to you at the beginning about using your self-authority? You decide which parts of this Skilled Empath Merge you will choose to remember.*

Of Course, Your Tact Can Grow

Telling your Discovery Person about the results of a Skilled Empath Merge — you have come such a long way, even to be thinking like this.

Take a moment to congratulate yourself, Awakening Empath. Those old unskilled empath merges required no tact whatsoever. Most of the information you received was kept secret even from your own conscious mind.

Although sharing with your Discovery Person can feel awkward at first, you can definitely develop the tact of a skilled empath. In fact, you have already taken a big step forward, just reading this chapter. Now you are fully prepared to explore the first of a long, thrilling sequence of techniques for flying in spirit.

CHAPTER 6

My Favorite Technique for Skilled Empath Merge

Thanks, John, Paul, George, and Ringo, for one of the greatest Beatles songs ever!

And speaking of gratitude, Awakening Empath, you may also be grateful that no singing is required for this first technique to do Skilled Empath Merge. It is my favorite and may well become a favorite of yours.

"I Want to Hold Your Hand" can really jet-propel your consciousness. Instantly your awareness will flow inside another person's body and aura. While in the midst of your empath merge, every feeling, thought, texture... every perception... every single thing you notice, even, about yourself... will count as information about your Discovery Person.

Of course, such experiences are subtle, not surfacey. As your sense of identity becomes well established, it will become increasingly easy to notice the contrast: Being yourself normally versus what happens for the short period of time while in Skilled Empath Merge.

Before techniquing, double check that you have done all this:

- You have invited your Discovery Person to receive a brief empath merge, to be discussed afterwards, planning for an approximate time of 10 minutes.
- Your Discovery Person accepted this invitation. Now the two of you are in a private location with your partner. Distractions have been prevented.

⁓ Recording equipment, like pen and paper, is within easy reach. (Same as these instructions!*")*

Explain what will happen next:

For this technique I will prepare, then open my eyes and hold hands as with a handshake — only without the up-and-down part. Next I will make some notes. (Silence will be appreciated until I have finished the technique.) Afterwards I will share some observations.

Feeling really bold? Add, "*I think you're going to enjoy this.*"

Then just one bit of preparation remains. You have already learned about how to practice the position. Let's refine the general idea:

Stand opposite your Discovery Person. Hold your partner's right hand as if preparing to shake hands, only don't add the shaking motion.

⁓ *Is your grip comfortable? Adjust as needed. Also, check to see if your arm itself has bent at an awkward angle and change that, as appropriate.*

⁓ *Are both your hands touching palm to palm? If not, move into that kind of handshake position.*

⁓ *Look down at the hands, not at your partner's face or expression.*

⁓ *Once your practice is done, let go.*

While you are officially in technique, this will be the position to use. Your eyes will be closed right before, and also immediately afterwards.

Since you just practiced, your partner will remember what to do while in technique. You won't have to say a word. Just open your eyes, reach out your hand, and get into that handshake. Do this during the technique step called "ASSUME THE POSITION."

Technique. I WANT TO HOLD YOUR HAND

To be done ON PURPOSE, for a short amount of time *only* with a consenting partner, your Discovery Person.

1. Standing opposite your Discovery Person, think: "Technique begins." Close your eyes.

2. Gently pay attention to yourself in an easy and casual way. Be especially interested in your emotions right now. Name one or more. (These have names like "happy, sad, scared, angry.") Open your eyes. Write down this "Before Picture about Your Emotions." Close your eyes again.

3. Turn attention to your physical body. Notice how any random part of your body physically feels right now. Sure, this has names like "strong, sore, relaxed, fidgety, heavy." Open your eyes. Write down this "Before Picture about Your Physical Self." Close your eyes again.

4. Get Big.

5. Set an intention, e.g., "I am ready to learn about my partner."

6. Take three Vibe-Raising Breaths. Immediately return to normal breathing.

7. "Assume the position" for a minute or less. Everything you experience now is about your Discovery Person (as experienced through your human instrument). Allow yourself to gently explore what it is like to be you, thoughts and feelings you have about your Discovery Person, etc.

8. Find some words to summarize what you experienced. Open your eyes and record it, quick and easy.

9. Close your eyes again. Repeat Steps 2 and 3, only this time it will be your "After Picture." Remember to close your eyes after recording.

10. Think something like, "Hooray, I did great!" etc. Definitely think "Technique complete." Open your eyes and go back to "being normal."

Look over your notes and decide what to tell your Discovery Person. Reward him or her with some insights. Definitely thank your Discovery Person for helping you to develop your skills as an empath.

Congratulations! I hope your Discovery Person loved the experience. Regardless of the feedback received, what you just did represents a triumph for your developing skills as an empath.

A Tiny Techie Quiz

In case you're curious, here is a chance to think in a technical way about what you just did.

Answer the questions below, then scroll down for answers.

1. *Can you name which steps of this technique were part of your Preparation Process?*

2. *Which steps of the technique hastened the re-entry into your very human sense of identity?*

3. *How much of this procedure counted for Official Technique Time?*

A Tiny Techie Quiz. ANSWERS.

1. *Preparation Process was Steps 1-6*

2. *Reentry and integration were set in motion with Step 10.*

3. *How much counted as Official Technique Time? Steps 1-10.*

Basically, gathering the data counts as part of your day's Technique Time.

What doesn't count:

- ∽ Locating a Discovery Person.
- ∽ Practicing the position for a technique.
- ∽ Adding to your notes about what you experienced, after Step 10.
- ∽ Deciding what to tell, and not tell, your Discovery Person.
- ∽ Communication time with your Discovery Person.
- ∽ Receiving praise, acknowledgement, cookies, etc. from a grateful Discovery Person (if applicable).

None of this counts as Official Technique Time. And this will be the same with every technique you learn for Skilled Empath Merge. Awakening Empath, as you gain experience, your respect may grow for essential components of every technique that *do* and *don't* count as Official Technique Time.

In the technique you just did, which steps were *not* part of the Preparation Process or re-entry? Only Steps 7 and 8. This will be similar for techniques other than "I Want to Hold Your Hand." The fancy, fun part of a Skilled Empath Merge amounts to a very small portion of the technique.

Well, did you know that DNA for all human beings is pretty similar? Geneticists say that only 1% of a person's DNA is distinctively individual. Small percentages can have big implications! For "I Want to Hold Your Hand," those non-distinctive parts help to highlight the amazing part.

Q&A. I Want to Hold Your Hand

Q. *Hey, doing that technique is as close as I have ever come to my childhood dream of being an astronaut. How did I do that?*

A. You used a technique to safely turn your empath gifts ON. The Preparation Process positioned your consciousness appropriately. When you added technique steps specific to "I Want to Hold Your Hand," this worked like a power launch for your consciousness.

Q. *I'm turning to this part of the Program for Empath Empowerment after several months. Actually I have been enjoying my life as a skilled empath with just Parts One and Two of this Program, knowing enough about my gifts to appreciate them. And then I have been keeping my empath gifts turned OFF.*

When I tried this technique a few months ago, quite frankly, I didn't enjoy it. I didn't notice much. I didn't like how it made me feel afterwards, either.

Until today I wasn't bothering with the Part Three aspect of turning my empath gifts ON. That's why I was absolutely amazed at how intense my experience was when I tried this technique again. Why is "I Want to Hold Your Hand" so much better now, quite a long time after I first became skilled as an empath?

A. Interesting question. On the whole, your mind-body-spirit system works more efficiently now. It's a big deal, not having empath gifts switched on at random for Split-Split-Second Empath Merges. When doing a Skilled Empath Merge this time, your everyday sense of self was stronger than before, right?

Q. *Exactly. That is why it seems so odd that I would travel in consciousness like some kind of astronaut. Why wouldn't the opposite happen? Why wouldn't I feel more stuck, since now I am living as myself (and loving it)?*

A. Empath gifts work better when used properly. A dedicated technique for Skilled Empath Merge directed your gifts appropriately. This became more noticeable now because you had broken the old pattern of unintentionally misusing those gifts.

By way of analogy, suppose that you had a washing machine. Somehow you never learned to turn it on properly. Instead you developed the habit of setting your washer for just the very last part of the rinse cycle.

Not a great way to wash clothes! You would have had to compensate for it somehow or other, like washing your clothes in the sink and figuring that your washing appliance might eventually be good for something else, but who knew what?

Suppose that eventually you felt ready to give your washing machine a new chance. You had a mechanic come to tune up your machine, get it working properly. Plus the mechanic taught you how to load that washer, set the controls properly, and do the full wash-and-rinse cycle that your appliance was designed to deliver.

In this analogy, your months of "no empath merge" helped to tune up your machine. And without your having to hire a mechanic, other than Mother Nature. By following the steps for "I Want to Hold Your Hand," you could finally experience what your empath gifts were designed to do.

Q. *Unlike that happy empath who just asked you questions, I didn't get more than I bargained for. I got a big fat nothing. Without being rude, are you and the other people here kidding? This isn't a technique for travel.*

A. What did happen?

Q. *To be honest, I felt really stupid, pretending to be going anywhere. The only thing I noticed was that, for a minute, I felt heavy and kind of constipated and worse than normal. This made me extremely uncomfortable. I sure hope that's not the glorious kind of thing you call "Otherness." Was it? Yuck.*

A. You have raised some important points. Otherness doesn't necessarily make you feel glorious, not unless you're swapping bodies with someone who feels inwardly like a king or queen.

Other people's strengths and problems are not necessarily the same as yours. Reflecting what just happened, it's pretty amazing how you could explore another person's inner experience at will, even if that means "Heavy and constipated." And perhaps even "Feeling stupid."

Eventually you will enjoy how the Otherness of another person's experience can be totally different from your expectations. This can become a glorious adventure!

Q. *I can relate to that last question. Probably I could tell you 100 things that didn't happen for every one that did. How can we sort the wheat from the chaff when doing a Skilled Empath Merge?*

A. Aha! Language comes to your rescue. When describing your experience, talk only about what happened that interested you. Ignore the rest.

Think of what happens when a baby learns to walk. Parents coo over the time their precious poppet lands upright. They don't rehash each of the 500 times he falls. That's smart. If all his parents did was criticize, it could take little Joshua 20 years before he mastered walking.

Reinforce your empath talent as if you were being your own good parent. Don't make a big deal about anything except for what interests you. Gradually, interesting experiences will happen more often and become increasingly vivid.

Q. *Talk about embarrassing experiences! I'm a woman, right, and I did my Skilled Empath Merge with a man. I absolutely loved being in a male body. But now I'm starting to worry. Could this mean that I'm gay?*

A. Don't worry. Skilled Empath Merge will not change your sexual orientation, whatever it is. If anything, you may have just demonstrated to yourself that you like having sex with men.

Of course, you may find it equally interesting to do Skilled Empath Merge with a woman. And without feeling the tiniest obligation to have sex with her, necessarily.

Meanwhile, isn't it interesting how men and women have such different ways of being in their bodies? Vive la difference!

Skilled Empath Merge can provide a unique form of sex education.

CHAPTER 7

Deep Listening

Skilled Empath Merge with "Deep Listening" is an altogether different technique for experiencing Otherness.

A new factor will be the launch location for your consciousness. Actually, make that two possible launch locations, because you will have a choice.

- ∾ The regular version of this technique has the launch pad located at the part of your client's body corresponding to the Heart Chakra.

- ∾ A variation gives you the option of launching your consciousness from a more commonly touched body part that also connects energetically to human emotions. Either choice will allow your emotional listening to go very deep.

So "Deep Listening" can deliver an experience of special interest if you are interested in your Discovery Person's emotional experiences. When you explore, it will be a plus if your gifts as an empath include either Emotional Oneness or Emotional Intuition or both. Yet this way to fly in spirit yields rich insights even if you have neither such gift.

How come? Like any technique for Skilled Empath Merge, "Deep Listening" is designed to engage every one of the empath gifts you do have. So get ready for some big fun, Awakening Empath.

Prepare Your Research Tool for Deep Listening

You will be using one ear for this technique. Which one? Your **DEEP LISTENING EAR.** This means whichever ear is better for listening energetically at depth.

Often a technique for Skilled Empath Merge requires the use of a RESEARCH TOOL: One part of your body is repurposed for flow-through with consciousness. Combine this with a dedicated technique for Skilled Empath Merge. Then a built-in component of your mind-body-spirit system… will become a launching device to fly in spirit.

For "Deep Listening," that Research Tool will be your Deep Listening Ear.

So which ear is it? Imagine that you are talking on a mobile phone or some other device that must be held up to one ear at a time. Further, imagine that you are talking to someone who matters a lot to you. When this person you care about is talking, the words are very important.

Okay, lift up one hand as if holding your phone to that ear.

Now, notice which ear that is. Whichever ear — that one — qualifies as your Deep Listening Ear. Use that Research Tool for this next technique of Skilled Empath Merge.

Practice Position #1 for "Deep Listening"

Whenever you do this technique, you can choose from two positions. The first will give you a clearer experience.

What's the catch? You will be placing your ear on your Discovery Person's chest or breasts, right in front of the breastbone. Will that be okay with *you*? If not, skip over to Practice Position #2.

If Position #1 is fine with you, find out if *your partner* will also be comfortable with this position. For instance, you might say:

This technique for Skilled Empath Merge is called 'Deep Listening.' A choice of physical position will be used, so let's practice that in advance of my actually doing the technique. Either way, the empath merge will work fine.

Is it okay with you if we do the version where I put my ear here? (Tap your own chest a few times.) Or would you prefer a hand position? (Gesture by lifting one hand up, giving one of your palms a little wave.)

If the heart-area position works for you and your partner, here is how to practice it.

1. Remember which is your Primary Listening Ear. *Stand in front of your Discovery Person. Figure out the approximate breastbone-level position.*

2. *On a guy, that's easy to find: Between his nipples.*

3. *On a gal, also seek out the breastbone area at the lowest part of the sternum, about an inch above where the ribs come together.*

When asked to "Assume the Position," you will be placing your ear right there.

Your next factor in positioning involves whether there might be a significant height difference between your partner and you.

Will you be able to place your ear in that position without standing on tiptoe or bending over a lot? You might ask your partner to sit on a chair. Or perhaps *you* might need a chair, so you can stand on it. It can be fun to work out logistics until they are comfortable for you both.

Then practice Position #1 for Deep Listening. Briskly position your ear. For now, keep your eyes open. Later, for part of the technique, your eyes will also be open. During the travel portion of "Deep Listening," your eyes will be closed.

Once position practice is done, move away from your partner. Check that your writing supplies are within easy reach, as are the steps to this technique. Excellent! You're ready to go.

Practice Position #2 for "Deep Listening"

The palm of your Discovery Person's hand can work beautifully for this Skilled Empath Merge. Which palm, though?

Make your choice based on this:

- ⌁ When your Deep Listening Ear is the left ear, choose the left hand of your Discovery Person.
- ⌁ When your Deep Listening Ear is the right ear, choose your Discovery Person's right hand.
- ⌁ Describing further how the two of you prepare for this technique, I'll call this appropriate hand of your partner's the RESEARCH HAND.

Ask your Discovery Person to stand with that Research Hand palm outward, facing toward you, holding that arm out to the side. Have your partner straighten that elbow.

Next comes your part of this research position. Your back will be to your partner's face, preventing the distraction of your looking at each other while you move in and out of Skilled Empath Merge.

Sure, your Discovery Person may (or may not) choose to stare at the back of your head. Who cares?

Firmly place your ear at the palm of your Discovery Person's Research Hand. Adjust the height of that palm by pulling your partner's straight arm up or down.

For practical purposes, that angle does not matter so long as your partner's arm remains straight. What does matter? Keep your head and neck at a comfortable angle.

When touching your ear to your partner's hand, does your neck feel comfortable? Also, is your chin even, rather than tilted up or down?

Excellent! Practice this position with your eyes open, then closed, then open again. This is how you will "Assume the position" for this technique of Skilled Empath Merge.

With practice complete, you can separate physically from your partner and stand normally. Check that your writing supplies are within easy reach, as are the steps to this technique. Excellent!

Technique. DEEP LISTENING

To be done on purpose, for a short time only, with a consenting partner. Awakening Empath, you have set aside the time, prevented distractions. Recording equipment is handy, and you have practiced the position. Preview the following steps in advance of doing this technique. Okay, you're good to go.

1. Standing opposite your partner, think: "Technique begins." Close eyes.

2. Gently pay attention to yourself in an easy and casual way. Be especially interested in your emotions right now. Name one or more.(These have names like "happy, sad, scared, angry.") Open your eyes. Write down this "Before Picture about Your Emotions." Close your eyes again.

3. Turn attention to your physical body. Notice how any random part of your body physically feels right now. Sure, this has names like "strong, sore, relaxed, fidgety, heavy." Open your eyes. Write down this "Before Picture about Your Physical Self." Close your eyes again.

4. Get Big

5. Set an intention, e.g., "I am ready to learn about my partner."

6. Take three Vibe-Raising Breaths. Immediately return to normal breathing. "Assume the position" for a minute or less. (Open your eyes long enough to get into position and then close them again.) Everything you experience now is about your partner through your human instrument, language, etc. Allow yourself to gently explore what it is like to be you, thoughts and feelings that you have about your Discovery Person, etc.

7. Find some words to summarize what you experienced. Open your eyes and quickly record it.

8. Close your eyes again. Repeat Steps 2 and 3 to record your "After Picture." Remember to close your eyes after you do that scribble writing.

9. Think something like, "Hooray, I did great!" etc. Definitely think "Technique complete." Open your eyes and return to "being normal."

Look over your notes and decide what to tell your Discovery Person. Reward him or her with some insights. Be sure to thank your Discovery Person for helping you to develop more skill as an empath.

Congratulations! I hope your Discovery Person loved the experience. Regardless of that feedback, consider what you just did a personal triumph of learning. Awakening Empath, you're on your way to becoming a Master Empath.

Q&A. Deep Listening

Q. *Well, who knew I could travel so far by listening to somebody else's palm! When I opened my eyes again, I was surprised to find myself in the room and breathing inside my own body. Where did I go, exactly?*

A. You were identifying with an experience of yourself as consciousness. Then that consciousness merged with the aura, or consciousness, of your partner.

When the technique ended, you went back to identifying with your body and surroundings, returning to your usual sense of self (with consciousness in the background). Now you can appreciate why one name for a dedicated empath merge is "Flying in spirit."

Q. *Was I supposed to focus on my Discovery Person's heartbeat? Because I'm not sure that I heard it.*

A. Regardless of whether or not you heard a heartbeat, everything about your experience counted. That's right. Every single thing you experienced during technique Step 6 counted.

Any future experiences will be similar: Pure improvisation. All that counts is what happens during Step 6. At that time, everything you feel or think or see or hear or know... that really does count as information about your Discovery Person.

Q. *When I connected, I heard a baby crying. Should I tell my partner what that meant to me? Or is it better just to say what I heard?*

A. When you're new to sharing your comments with a partner, you might prefer to offer the raw material, e.g., "I heard a baby crying. Does this mean anything to you?"

However, as you grow more comfortable with Flying in Spirit, you will find an interpretation that feels right intuitively. There's no problem with offering this so long as you phrase it with humility.

Q. *What do you mean by "Phrase it with humility"?*

A. Suppose that, when you heard the sound of the crying baby, the underlying feeling reminded you of your frustration as a new mother. You might say, "I experienced frustration, like when I was a new mother and I didn't know how to cope. Does this have anything to do with your feelings right now?"

Q. *As opposed to saying what?*

A. "You have an Inner Child who is crying his heart out. You should heal your Inner Child."

Q. *Is empath talent about giving people advice like that?*

A. Definitely not! It is not appropriate for words from a Skilled Empath Merge to be diagnostic, coercive, judgmental, or deterministic, e.g., "You should." "You're bad." "You are supposed to."

Q. *I have studied your system of Aura Reading Through All Your Senses®. There I learned to interpret my immediate perceptions and only share interpretations with a partner. Are you saying that Skilled Empath Merge can be different?*

A. Exactly. With an empath merge, it is fine to say, "I experienced x, y, z." Whereas the aura reading skills that I teach have you interpret any immediate perception before sharing it.

I define aura reading as your perception plus your interpretation. The way I teach skills of energetic literacy, only your interpretation counts for aura reading.

Skilled Empath Merge is different. Sometimes you will tactfully share your perception, your experience. Other times you will find a clear and spontaneous interpretation, which you would tell to your Discovery Person (rather than your initial perception). Your choice.

Being more personal, your experience as an empath can sometimes be an image or emotion or physical sensation. Share that, if you feel comfortable doing so.

Q. *Otherwise?*

A. Otherwise, keep that part of your findings private. You are learning how to become a tactful empath, right? After you scribble-write your notes, look them over. Be selective about what you choose to tell your Discovery Person.

Q. *How else is Skilled Empath Merge different from aura reading? Of course, there are many different ways to read auras. I'm asking about the way that you teach aura reading, as a form of energetic literacy rather than psychic development.*

A. Skilled Empath Merge brings a deeper degree of insight.

Also, the process of gathering information feels more personal. You are fortunate to be an empath, whatever your gifts. Because Skilled Empath Merge is a form of deeper perception that only 1 in 20 people can do, whereas everybody can learn to read auras.

Q. *I feel really terrible now. Guess I chose the wrong person to try this technique on. How could I have known in advance?*

A. There is a certain art to choosing a partner for Skilled Empath Merge. Pay as much attention as you would before crossing a street. Rather than blindly rushing in, take a minute to ask inside, "Is it wise for me to join empathically with this person?"

Intuitively we always know the truth about partnering choices. Carl Rogers, the great psychologist, found that people who meet with a new therapist can tell within minutes whether or not that particular therapist will be able to help them. When people disregard their inner turnoff, they can spend years in therapy with very limited success.

Q. *Then what do you tell a person who turns you off, "No way"?*

A. Bring back your best manners from high school dances. When an unwanted partner asks you to dance, you don't have to sock him in the jaw. Simply say, "Not now, thanks."

Besides, at this stage in your development as a skilled empath, please don't put yourself in the position of allowing people to demand energetic readings. You are the one to issue the invitation. Deciding whether to approach a Discovery Person can be just like crossing a street — something you figure out before making your move.

Q. *Shortly after doing Step 6. I felt scared and wanted to come back to my body right away. So I dropped my partner's hand and opened my eyes. Now I feel anxious. What did I do wrong?*

A. Stopping the technique was smart. You always have the right to come out of an empath merge. Only it's preferable to come out properly, rather than just opening your eyes. Otherwise you could feel rough for a while. Here are instructions for a smoother re-entry.

Technique. EMERGENCY DISCONNECT FROM SKILLED EMPATH MERGE

Almost always, it will be enjoyable doing a technique for Skilled Empath Merge. If you're not having a great time, let go any physical position you may have been using for the technique. And if you were recording your experiences, stop. Even mid-sentence.

If you were physically touching your Discovery Person, let go. Look away. Notice at least one physical object. Then:

1. Close your eyes.

2. Choose inwardly to bring full awareness back inside your body. Feel your body fill up with pure YOU-ness. Or, to put it another way, notice how it feels physically to be you.

3. Take a moment to give thanks inwardly for what you experienced with the technique. (Sure, you received more than you bargained for, but you can still feel some gratitude for an educational experience.)

4. Take 11 Grounding Breaths.

5. Open your eyes, taking plenty of time. Say out loud, "I choose to psychically disconnect from my partner. I have strong, clear energetic boundaries."

Q. *If my Discovery Person is nearby, is it okay if I just whisper that last part?*

A. Sure.

Q. *What am I supposed to tell that Discovery Person? "Sorry, nothing to tell you. Because you were way too freaky."*

A. Thank the person for helping you. Say that you're still learning how to do this technique, and this has added to your experience. Conversation over.

Q. *If your partner presses for details, what then?*

A. Perhaps explain a bit. Say that you have just begun doing empath merges, and it takes some getting used to before you are really smooth with it. Thank your partner. Done!

Rest assured, this sort of problem almost never comes up. I'm offering you a strategy for the very remote possibility that you might not feel comfortable doing an empath merge with a particular person.

Q. *I enjoyed my first time doing "Deep Listening." But what did I really give my Discovery Person? I felt foolish just sharing how she seemed to me as a person.*

A. You gave the gift of validation. From childhood on, we love to see ourselves through the appreciative eyes of another person. Reality checks come in many forms. An empath's wise, clear feedback is one of the greatest gifts ever.

PART TWO

Advanced Empath Merge

Skilled Empath Merge is not flashy. You'll have to settle for human, gently self-actualizing, and natural.

Awakening Empath, you have begun to experience this. Now that you have experimented with your first techniques to fly in spirit, you're in a better position to understand why I drew a certain distinction back in *The Empowered Empath*. Remember this idea? "What does being an empath have to do with psychic ability? Exactly nothing."

And how about this? "Psychic experience adds to your collection of information, while Skilled Empath Merge changes the knower."

Truth expands, based on experience. By now you can appreciate, better than ever, how Skilled Empath Merge could be compared to a long-term love relationship. Day by day, year after year, one adventure at a time, you learn about that other person's distinctive who-you-be.

Don't expect this to feel like *falling in love*, either. It's a deepening, as happens with a love that endures.

What is the secret pleasure of every skilled empath? We can explore deepening with *every* person we choose, not just one special relationship (however delightful). Moreover, we can explore without lifestyle complications or broken hearts.

It's this simple, Awakening Empath: One Skilled Empath Merge at a time, you can explore anybody you choose. Probe into the specialness of that person who fascinates you. And you won't be complicating your life with the equivalent of a harem. Enjoy, then go forth and explore your next Discovery Person. Then the next.

As if you had the right to do so! Because you *are* allowed. You were born as an empath.

With skill, you can use your empath gifts for the purpose intended:

- So long as you keep those empath gifts OFF most of the time.
- So long as you keep your lifestyle in balance, doing just that 20 daily minutes of Official Technique Time, maximum.
- Unobtrusively you can explore, to your heart's content, any Discovery Person of interest to you.

And now, Awakening Empath, you are ready for **ADVANCED EMPATH MERGE,** ultra-sophisticated techniques for depth exploration of Otherness... while you remain protected and balanced as yourself.

CHAPTER 8

The Sight Worth More Than 1,000 Words

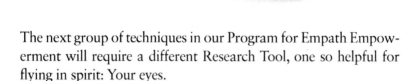

The next group of techniques in our Program for Empath Empowerment will require a different Research Tool, one so helpful for flying in spirit: Your eyes.

Supposedly a picture is worth a thousand words. Well, this new way of using your vision can deliver something far more valuable than the proverbial thousand words.

Long before developing empath skills, you found many ways to engage with people through vision. Before going into this new-and-special use for vision, let's take a quick survey. Have any of the following been favorite ways for you to use your eyes?

1. SURVIVAL MODE, where you are watching objective reality. Here, Awakening Empath, you notice practical details like the name of the street, whether anybody there seems dangerous, how to reach your destination without getting lost.

2. ARTISTIC MODE, which allows a certain agreeable kind of space-out, so you can revel in colors or shapes or designs... like the born artist you are.

3. BEAUTY PAGEANT MODE, as if you have been chosen to rank the physical attributes of each person parading before you. Who wins, and what's the name for that contest? "The Swimsuit Competition" or what?

4. SOCIAL STATUS MODE, where you critique a woman's makeup or a man's mustache. Or perhaps you evaluate an entire outfit, deconstructing every bit of social symbolism.

5. PHYSIOGNOMY. Observing a person's most intriguing items of physical face data, you employ face reading skills to interpret the significance.

6. GAZING. For this you might use a soft receptive focus, totally open to whatever you see — perhaps in the manner of watching a favorite TV show — only you're doing this while engaged in real life.

7. UH-OH. The unblinking stare that you used to have while slip-sliding into Prolonged Empath Merge. Whew, Awakening Empath, not something that you do any more, right?

In order for your eyes to serve as a tool with Skilled Empath Merge, you will use them differently from any of these seven uses. This different use is a hidden potential for empaths, secret and super-simple, yet fascinating.

Remember how you have connected to your Discovery Person in previous techniques? You used a Research Tool. Already you have done "Practice the Position" with two different ones:

- Your Handshake Hand as a Research Tool
- Your Deep Listening Ear as a Research Tool

Now, Awakening Empath, it's time to learn how to develop a TRUTH SIGHT RESEARCH TOOL. Fair warning, this will be different from all those seven ways mentioned previously.

Technique. FIND YOUR TRUTH SIGHT RESEARCH TOOL

Awakening Empath, simply read the following teaching sequence, then do it. Since this is not a technique for Skilled Empath Merge, there will be no Preparation Process. However, you would be wise to take the usual precautions to avoid interruptions, refrain from multi-tasking, etc.

In the following sequence, I will refer to "The floor." Of course, that could be carpet, wood, dirt, whatever. No need to seek out fancy flooring before you can activate your eyes in this special, new way.

I will also refer to "Your feet." Are your feet wearing shoes right now or bare? Are you wearing socks with clocks? Whatever. You know which body part I mean.

Simplicity itself — it can be so easy learning how to transform your eyes into a TRUTH SIGHT RESEARCH TOOL. Allow five minutes for this little treat.

1. Sit so that your feet make contact with the floor. If they don't quite reach, find a firm pillow to place beneath them.

2. Bending over a bit, look down and visually locate your right foot.

3. See the floor to your right. Then see the floor in front of you.

4. Now view your left foot. Next, look at the floor to the left of that foot.

5. Find your lap area. See the base of your torso. (If you're wearing pants, creases at each thigh make this easy to spot.)

6. In the room where you are, locate a corner at the ceiling. Then find a corner by the floor. Can you find a third corner in a different part of the room?

7. Okay, back to your body. Look down and see your belly.

8. Choose any random physical object in front of you. Watch that briefly.

9. Okay, let's return to your body. Bend over a bit and see your midriff, that area above the waist, framed by ribs on either side. What you can't see all of it? No problem. Just see some of it. Good enough.

10. For a change of scene, visually survey the ceiling. No fancy looking required. Don't search for biblical figures unless you're in a place painted like the Sistine Chapel.

11. Look down and see your chest or breasts.

12. Stretch all over, not particularly looking at anything. Technique over. Automatically your eyes will revert to other uses.

Congratulations, Awakening Empath. You have succeeded at using your eyes as a Truth Sight Research Tool.

Dramatically different from other ways of looking? Not really. This a simple way of aiming your eyes. Simpler than normal, in fact. Yet oh-so-useful, as you will soon discover!

Q&A: Find Your Truth Sight Research Tool

Q. *That was fun. I guess you could say I was good at it. Doesn't seem like a big deal, though. What on earth did all that have to do with positioning consciousness?*

A. That physical body of yours is miraculous as a way to direct consciousness. Every adult human is built with a huge range of consciousness-related capabilities.

And lucky you, being an empath! Your capabilities include making a shift in consciousness into the energy field of another person, then directly experiencing what it is like to be that person.

Moving your eyes to look, simply look, is not a technique for Skilled Empath Merge. However, this can be used *during* techniques in this Program for Empath Empowerment.

You have just practiced using your eyes to look at, or locate, one part of your body at a time. This meant directing your eyes with simple awareness, without engaging other abilities but simply connecting visually. Which is exactly how to use your eyes as a tool for Skilled Empath Merge.

Q. *What was the point of looking at things other than my body?*

A. Many empaths have the habit of looking ever-deeper, striving to learn more, seldom taking objective reality at surface value.

By contrast, you just experimented with an easy, sloppy technique. Un-self-consciously, you positioned physical vision (and thus your consciousness) at surface-level reality.

Alternating between different body parts and inanimate objects helped you remember to look in a particular way. You were reminded that you can do something which *non-empaths* do very often, keeping awareness superficial.

Q. *I'm curious. Why did you have us look at our feet?*

A. Symbolically, feet support human individuality. Consciousness will subtly shift when you move your eyes there. Every part of the body has symbolic meaning that can position consciousness in a particular way.

You see, consciousness can be positioned by *where* we look at someone's body as well as *how* we look. *Moving* specific body parts can further position consciousness, as with the age-old mystical techniques of tai chi and yoga. As a humble variation, expressly designed for this Program for Empath Empowerment, here is an energetic workaround that employs your Truth Sight Research Tool and also your feet.

Learn How to "Shallow Up"

This energetic workaround is named in honor of skilled empath Astrit Wold, my Norwegian student who came up with the brilliant terminology SHALLOW UP! This means, "Stop going deeper into experience. No slip-sliding into unskilled empath merges. Right now, position your consciousness back at the surface of life."

Workaround. SHALLOW UP QUICKIE

The following technique is accomplished rapidly, and it takes your awareness right up to the surface of life. So you don't need to count this as Official Technique Time. Use this workaround as one more way to turn your empath gifts OFF:

1. If you start floating off, flying in spirit, take a moment to look at your feet.

2. Then look at a part of the room, like a wall. Look back at your feet.

3. Automatically, your awareness will be re-positioned at the level of your physical body. This works very fast, like refreshing a computer screen.

Perhaps this tiny technique will remind you of another resource you have learned for keeping your empath gifts OFF, "Introduction to Grounding Breaths" from *The Empowered Empath*.

As with that other technique, please do not add optional steps, such as telling yourself "Now I am supposed to feel grounded." Get the difference?

Now, Awakening Empath, let's return to discussing "Find Your Truth Sight Research Tool."

Q. *What about those other body parts that you had us look at? Why choose those particular parts of the body?*

A. Each one corresponds to a major chakra.

   ⟿ Your Root Chakra is where your legs come together.
   ⟿ You Belly Chakra is beneath your navel.
   ⟿ Your Solar Plexus Chakra is at the midriff area.
   ⟿ Your Heart Chakra is at the breastbone.

All these corresponding body parts are pretty easy to see on yourself, even without a mirror.

Some advanced techniques for Skilled Empath Merge will require that you direct consciousness towards a particular chakra area on yourself or a Discovery Person. Later!

Q. *Wow, the chakras! So should I start visualizing red at the Root Chakra and orange at the Belly Chakra, etc., as I have been taught?*

A. Please, spare yourself. Do not add any techniques from outside this Program for Empath Empowerment. This would be counter-productive.

For "Find Your Truth Sight Research Tool" were you able to use your eyes in the simplest way possible, just looking at one thing rather than another?

Q. *Sure. But wasn't that really ridiculously basic? Can't we do something more sophisticated if we're more advanced in our knowledge of chakras?*

A. The most advanced students of spirituality and energy have learned to be humble. Good for you, that you didn't let other skills and random bits of information sabotage using your Truth Sight Research Tool for Skilled Empath Merge.

While flying in spirit, whenever you use this Research Tool, please maintain a similar simplicity. Looking connects you to the Discovery Person. Later on, when a technique invites you to explore a particular chakra area, you will be directing consciousness at a certain part of the person's body, like the chest or belly. Regular, simple human vision is plenty.

In all our techniques for Skilled Empath Merge, you never will get better results if you attempt to see energy or feel something paranormal. By keeping your technique simple and human, you'll grow faster, too.

Still, many of you empaths may be wondering about the language of metaphysics, like chakras and seeing colors, so let's explore that in our next chapter.

CHAPTER 9

Taking a Selfie with Empath Merge

Awakening Empath, you have learned to use your eyes as a Truth Sight Research Tool for Skilled Empath Merge. Now I'll coach you to direct that at yourself, courtesy of a mirror.

Will this involve clairvoyance? Now that's a good question.

Mirror-viewing habits can vary enormously. Remember, in our last chapter, we considered seven different ways to use vision. Then you began to use eyesight as a Truth Sight Research Tool. To employ this on yourself, it helps to understand that you have three very different options for self-viewing.

1. Taking a *casual, surface-level* look at yourself in the mirror.

2. *Aiming for ultimate significance,* perhaps a grand and portentous clairvoyant view of yourself in a mirror.

3. Seeking something in-between, maybe more humble: *A deeper truth* — at least *some* of the deeper truth — about yourself, courtesy of a mirror.

Let's distinguish these three options further. The differences matter a lot for becoming a Master Empath.

Three Very Different Ways to Use in a Mirror

Some expectations can distort our experience. Other expectations can make us feel dissatisfied when doing a technique, even though the results we got were perfect (even wonderful). To prevent disappointment let's compare and contrast three very different expectations for looking in the mirror.

Version #1. Business as usual, using today's technology

Living when you do, how rare a treat does it seem when you can gaze into a mirror? Not such a big deal, is it? Because you live more than 200 years after silver-backed mirrors were invented.

Do you realize how different it has been throughout most of human history? Learning how you looked to others was really hard. What if the closest you could come was to hunt down a still pond in warm weather and give yourself a long, hard squint? On a day when that worked fairly well, you might stop and think something like this:

A heavenly experience has just been vouchsafed unto me. For behold! I am now able to witness my own reflection, even as others might see me. This heavenly vision, worthy of an aristocrat, is unforgettable. And thus the memory of encountering this looking glass will be consecrated within my bosom as a perpetual reminder to comport myself gracefully. May I walk henceforth on a path of righteousness.

Nah. What's more likely? Mirror technology doesn't strike you as the least bit advanced. You will grab a look for the purpose intended. Could be as mundane as checking if any food is caught between your teeth.

Though ordinary, a quick look in the mirror can still prove reassuring. One quick glimpse can steady your everyday sense of self.

Not so bad. See that? I still have this head. It still is attached to the rest of my body. Life goes on.

Whether for keeping track of body parts or basic hygiene, this quick-and-casual use of a mirror does something to consciousness. Automatically your awareness zooms right to the surface of life, regular human frequencies related to the conscious mind. You shallow up and perceive at life's surface, objective reality.

Yes, Awakening Empath, once again I'm reminding you of a big-deal, though subtle point, about positioning your consciousness.

This matters because consciousness serves as your basic equipment for flying in spirit. Really it is astounding how moving any part of your body physically... can alter your positioning of consciousness.

Our next technique for Skilled Empath Merge will make use of this quick-and-casual way of physically looking at something, at anything.

Please do not try to fancy up how you do quick-and-casual. (Isn't it reassuring to find an area in life where squinting is not required?) Frankly, you already know plenty about regular looking in a mirror.

Version #2. Oooh, clairvoyance

The Latin name simply means *clear sight*. But wow, such associations! CLAIRVOYANCE is rife with pretty-pretty expectations of psychic flash, what I call "**THE ROMANCE OF THE ASTRAL.**"

Ooh, seeing yourself or somebody else, clairvoyantly? Sounds so special! Might that special gifted sight foretell the future? Perhaps angelic insights will be imparted, conveying celestial wisdom about what truly, ineffably matters.

That very word "clairvoyance" brings an otherworldly association. This might seem very appealing. Except let's get practical, Awakening Empath. What happens when you seek clairvoyant vision? Consciousness is positioned at the astral, those psychic-level frequencies corresponding to your subconscious mind.

Granted, you might choose to do this sometimes. It would count as part of your Official Technique Time.

Actually our next technique for Skilled Empath Merge will position consciousness, very briefly, at your subconscious frequencies.

Except there the similarity ends. Skilled Empath Merge never involves psychic development. That's like comparing apples and oranges.

In the technique that follows, you will not be consulting an astral guide, as psychic work is generally done. The "Get Big" technique in your Preparation Process will ensure that your consciousness teams up to co-create with Divine frequencies, corresponding to your Higher Self. Mostly you will be thinking, feeling, and scribble-writing — doing all of this as your everyday, regular self.

Version #3. Simply seeing the truth

TRUTH SIGHT: Seems to me, that name is just about right for what you're about to do. Not too little. Not too big. Just right.

After aiming your eyes, and doing a straightforward technique, you can learn about yourself or another Discovery Person. The ensuing knowledge will be human-level, bolstering your humanity, done in a safe way that protects you, preventing Imported STUFF.

Awakening Empath, this Version 3 for using your eyes is an empowering variation on Version 1. Doing this, you look in your mirror with an everyday naturalness, un-self-consciously.

All that will be different is your context for looking into the mirror. You will be in technique, using a *technique that positions consciousness* to help you find a deeper version of human truth.

Get the difference? Not using your eyes to find a deeper version of human truth. Using a technique for that purpose.

Of course, the usual caution applies. Like any technique for Skilled Empath Merge, either do the full technique or don't bother. No cheating!

Practice the Position

To prepare for "Self-Discovery with Truth Sight," stand in front of a full-length mirror (or another mirror that is, at least, long enough to clearly show your ribcage area).

Practice seeing the midriff part of your body — lower than the chest or breasts and higher than your waist. Move forwards and backwards until you find that sweet spot of mirror-gazing, where your ribcage area shows comfortably.

No need for special clothing to practice this position. Definitely do not remove clothing. That would prepare you for a different technique, perhaps work as a stripper.

Keep your writing equipment nearby, along with the steps for this next technique.

Now this next part might seem funny, Awakening Empath, but here goes: Practice standing in front of your mirror *without* looking directly ahead into the mirror. Instead look down or up or to the side.

You see, even while standing directly in front of a mirror, it is possible to avoid looking into it. For "Self-Discovery with Truth Sight," you will only look directly into the mirror during "Assume the position." That's when, spontaneously, you'll be using your Truth Sight Research Tool. The rest of your Technique Time, look elsewhere.

Technique. SELF-DISCOVERY WITH TRUTH SIGHT

Awakening Empath, you have set aside the time, prevented distractions. Recording equipment is handy, and you have practiced the position. Preview the following steps in advance of doing this technique. Then you're ready to go.

1. Stand in the position you have practiced, eyes open but not looking in the mirror. Think: "Technique begins." Close your eyes.

2. Gently pay attention to yourself in an easy and casual way. Be especially interested in your emotions right now. Name one or more. (These have names like "happy, sad, scared, angry.") Open your eyes. Write down this "Before Picture about Your Emotions." Close your eyes again.

3. Turn attention to your physical body. Notice how any random part of your body feels right now, physically. Sure, this has names like "strong, sore, relaxed, fidgety, heavy." Open your eyes. Write down this "Before Picture about Your Physical Self." Close your eyes again.

4. Get Big.

5. Set an intention, e.g., "I am ready to learn about myself."

6. Take three Vibe-Raising Breaths. Immediately return to normal breathing.

7. "Assume the position," aiming your Truth Sight Research Tool at your ribcage area. Keep eyes open for a minute or less, according to what feels comfortable to you, before you let your eyes close. Everything you experience now counts, so inwardly note whatever you experience as information, be it a thought or feeling, a physical sensation or an inner image.

8. Find some words to summarize what you experienced. Open your eyes and quickly record it.

9. Close your eyes again. Repeat Steps 2 and 3 to record your "After Picture."

10. Think something like, "Hooray, I did great!" etc. Definitely include "Technique complete." Open your eyes and go back to "Being normal."

Look over your notes and say the highlights aloud, as if speaking to someone you respect, even admire. Reward yourself with insights that came from seeing yourself with fresh eyes, your natural, human Truth Sight.

Q&A. Self-Discovery with Truth Sight

Q. *I'm curious about that quick-and-casual way of using my eyes. When I brush my teeth and look at myself, or I look at myself in the mirror at other times, will this now start to count as Official Technique Time? Please tell me no.*

A. No.

Granted, that quick-and-casual way of using your eyes is a way to move consciousness. Nevertheless, it does not qualify as your precious Technique Time.

You get a bonus for asking such a great question...

Workaround. ANOTHER SUPER-EASY WAY TO TURN YOUR EMPATH GIFTS OFF

A few moments of surfacey self-inspection, by means of a mirror, can help to keep your empath gifts turned OFF.

That simple. And how useful is that! Add this to your official collection of workarounds and techniques for life as a skilled empath: If you're feeling spacey, find a mirror and use it in a normal human way. Any mirror!

This need not be a special looking glass like the one in Snow White, famed for the notorious "Mirror, Mirror on the Wall" app. Here's the full workaround:

1. Find a regular mirror and look at yourself for a minute or so.
2. Admire those gorgeous eyes.
3. Check that no food is caught between your teeth.
4. Before going out in public, make sure you are wearing at least as much as a fig leaf, etc.

As a side effect, automatically, you will shallow up — with consciousness positioned at being you, the human, having a human life.

Now back to Q&A for that useful technique, "Self-Discovery with Truth Sight."

Q. *This empath technique with the mirror gave me a lot of information, and fast. But can I trust it?*

A. Of course. Think it over, now that you have finished "Self-Discovery with Truth Sight." Take whatever is useful and enjoy that part. No Skilled Empath Merge counts as a royal decree. (Besides, you may not live in a monarchy.)

Consider whatever you found as valuable information for you to use as you wish.

I congratulate you on exploring a new technique that will support your personal sense of self-authority.

Q. *I loved how that empath technique made me feel. Would it be alright if I do it off and on all day long?*

A. Not if you aim to live as a skilled empath! Remember, a skilled empath mostly keeps gifts turned OFF.

It's easy to protect your personal balance and emerging sense of identity. Include "Self-Discovery with Truth Sight" during your Official Technique Time. Otherwise, no-go.

Q. *But what if I'm stuck in a boring business meeting? What if I'm in line at the supermarket? This technique has made me fall in love with mirrors. What's to stop me from giving myself this special experience any time that I can see my reflection in a glass window or mirror?*

A. Nothing need stop you... except for good judgment. Empath talent can seem like a shiny new toy, especially now that you are learning techniques to mobilize it. But too much Technique Time can become as big a problem as constantly doing unskilled empath merges.

Remember the consequences of that, back in the day?

In boring situations, you can find other ways aplenty for amusing yourself, diversions that are based in everyday human reality. By reserving energetic explorations for your Official Technique Time, you will make the most of your empath gifts. What about the rest of the time? You can make the most of your life.

Q. *There has to be a way to do a variation on this technique to read other people. Can you teach us, pretty please?*

A. Definitely. Next!

CHAPTER 10

Truth Sight Expands

Awakening Empath, whoever thought you'd be taking a selfie with Advanced Empath Merge? That technique in our last chapter gave you access to an empath's view of yourself, so different from regular, everyday forms of introspection.

When you began keeping your empath gifts turned OFF, did it feel like deprivation? Was it hard for you, relinquishing the habit of unskilled empath merges all day long?

It is not unusual to feel empty or sad, getting used to living with your consciousness in "Solitary confinement."

Many empaths feel uncomfortable doing this for the first few weeks or months. Yet they persist. Eventually an empath can become well-adjusted to having your inner life be primarily about *you*.

By now, Awakening Empath, you have cleaned up your instrument for deeper perception. Quite apart from all the personal benefits of that stronger sense of identity, technically you are eligible to explore a variety of empath merge skills.

You cannot handshake yourself with "I Want to Hold Your Hand" nor insert your physical ear in front of your chest, as with the technique for "Deep Listening." So I'm glad you have learned how to research yourself by means of a simple mirror.

What if you wish to use your eyes as a tool for empathic research into a Discovery Person? If you feel ready to learn, I am ready to teach you. Right now. Let's prepare the basics involved in "Truth Sight for Advanced Empath Merge."

Prepare, then Practice the Position

Awakening Empath, prepare in these very human-reality ways to do this advanced form of Skilled Empath Merge:

- ∼ Invite your Discovery Person to receive a brief empath merge, which will be discussed afterwards. Total time commitment is about 10 minutes.
- ∼ After your Discovery Person accepts the invitation, make sure the two of you are in a private location.
- ∼ Prevent distractions there.
- ∼ Keep recording equipment handy, likewise instructions for the technique.

As preparation, what remains? Practice the physical position for "Truth Sight for Advanced Empath Merge."

1. Stand directly opposite your Discovery Person.

2. Preview more specifically what will happen: *I will do a brief inner preparation for this technique. Then I will open my eyes and look at your ribcage area. Next, I'll make some notes. Silence will be appreciated until I finish. Afterwards I will share what I learned about you, researching as an empath.*

3. Practice the physical position you will be using for "Assume the position." If your partner's arms or hands are placed over the torso, request that arms hang loose until you have finished doing the technique.

How precise must you be, aiming your Truth Sight Research Tool at your Discovery Person's ribcage area? That's above the waist and below the chest or breasts — a pretty large area.

So relax. Anywhere in that physical vicinity will work just fine.

Technique. TRUTH SIGHT FOR ADVANCED EMPATH MERGE

Awakening Empath, you have set aside the time, prevented distractions. Recording equipment is handy, and you have practiced the position. Preview the following steps in advance of doing this technique and away we go.

1. Standing opposite your Discovery Person, think: "Technique begins." Close your eyes.

2. Gently pay attention to yourself in an easy and casual way. Be especially interested in your emotions right now. Name one or more.(These have names like "happy, sad, scared, angry.") Open your eyes. Write down this "Before Picture about Your Emotions." Close your eyes again.

3. Turn attention to your physical body. Notice how any random part of your body physically feels right now. Sure, this has names like "strong, sore, relaxed, fidgety, heavy." Open your eyes. Write down this "Before Picture about Your Physical Self." Close your eyes again.

4. Get Big.

5. Set an intention, e.g., "I am ready to learn about my partner."

6. Take three Vibe-Raising Breaths. Immediately return to normal breathing.

7. "Assume the position," aiming your Truth Sight Research Tool at your Discovery Person's ribcage area. Keep eyes open for a minute or less, according to what feels comfortable to you, before you let your eyes close. Everything you experience now... will inform you about your Discovery Person in the here and now.

8. Find some words to summarize what you have noticed with emotions, physical sensations, images, words, energies. Open your eyes and quickly record it. Close your eyes again.

9. Repeat Steps 2 and 3 to record your "After Picture." Remember to close your eyes afterwards.

10. Think something like, "Hooray, I did great!" etc. Definitely include "Technique complete." Open your eyes and go back to "Being normal."

Look over your notes and speak the tactful parts aloud. Remember to thank your Discovery Person for helping you to develop your skills as an empath.

Q&A. Truth Sight for Advanced Empath Merge

Q. *The main thing I noticed was how different it was to be my Discovery Person, different compared to being myself. I know him very well. How come this time I noticed so many things that I never saw before?*

A. First off, give yourself credit for developing good habits with keeping your empath gifts turned OFF in everyday life. This adds to the contrast when you finally do Skilled Empath Merge.

Q. *Well, I'm not sure I deserve so much credit. You see, I have known Robert for 20 years and I have been married to him most of that time. That includes long before I started to learn Empath Empowerment.*

So I'm pretty sure I have been doing plenty of unskilled empath merges. I want to know, what made this experience so much more vivid than, even, all those years of unskilled empath merges?

A. Doing any dedicated technique for Skilled Empath Merge can bring you much clearer results. It is different from what you learn by living with a person, even from loving a person.

Skilled Empath Merge really does take you deeper, moving your awareness into temporary experience inside that person's energy field.

Usually this information is subconscious-level, not conscious. Vibrational frequencies there are astral, not human, of course.

Moreover, unlike any unskilled empath merges, you are experiencing through a technique that focuses your gifts and helps to produce maximum clarity.

Q. *In "The Empowered Empath," you explained about Prolonged Empath Merge, how that is unskilled but can last a lot longer than the split-split-second-type of empath merges. I get how "Truth Sight for Advanced Empath Merge" would bring more clarity than the split-split-second dealies, but why would it be more informative than one of the Prolonged Empath Merges?*

A. Let's make an analogy to singing. Suppose that you have a beautiful tenor voice. That's like having empath gifts — useful for this analogy because the voice is something innate, not a skill set.

Suppose that, often, in the past, you would be talking when your voice would unexpectedly hit some high notes. That wasn't giving a vocal performance, just that more of your vocal range happened to slip out.

This could be compared to doing some Split-Split-Second Empath Merges. Not on purpose and hardly like singing a song.

As that talented but untrained tenor, maybe you would sing some long notes as well. Little bits of a song. All this might sound pretty good but only hint at your full potential as a singer.

Like a Prolonged Empath Merge, sometimes your talent might show a bit more. This would further reveal your full potential as a singer. Like a hint of what you could do if you also developed good technique, real skill to supplement your natural talent.

Next, imagine that you study with a vocal coach, learning skills for breathing and vocal support. Afterwards you sing a song that lets your vocal gorgeousness show. The impact might be very different, right?

Well that is the difference between just having empath gifts versus using your talent along with a dedicated skill set that has been specifically designed to support you.

Q. *Why would my thoughts and feelings during Step 7 count as information about being my Discovery Person?*

A. "Truth Sight for Advanced Empath Merge" is a systematic technique designed to produce a specific result. If you follow the steps of the technique you will get the result.

Q. *But you don't understand. Here is one example of what crossed my mind in Step 7. I felt foolish, self-conscious, and awkward. I started doubting my ability to master the technique at all! What could this typical self-doubt possibly have to do with my Discovery Person?*

A. What makes you so sure those qualities of self-doubt were really about you? Textures of life experience, including the emotion of self-doubt, can be considered information about your Discovery Person.

Being human, you are unlikely to have abstract experiences. Far more often, you will place a bit of information, or texture of life experience, into the context of your everyday life.

Remember this general principle:

Whatever you experience during a Skilled Empath Merge... counts as information about your Discovery Person.

So "Feeling self-doubt" counts as information about your Discovery Person.

Similarly when you felt "foolish, self-conscious, and awkward," that also counted as information about your partner.

What if your Discovery Person had been brimming with self-esteem and self-confidence? Then you might have registered this texture of life experience as "I am really, really great at doing this technique. I'm amazing."

Q. *That's a very different way of understanding my experiences. Can you offer any suggestions for making that kind of leap, or detachment, or whatever is involved?*

A. Just keep doing the steps of whichever technique you are doing. Write down a quick summary. Don't worry if it feels personal, since many empath gifts do have a personal quality.

Simply write down whatever information you receive. After emerging from the technique, review what you recorded. When you review that recording (a form of objective reality), it can become easier to get outside your head and assess what happened.

Q. *My experience didn't seem personal at all, not like what she was just asking about. It was very obvious to me that everything I felt was about my Discovery Person. One of my empath gifts is Physical Intuition, so I even knew that there was some pain in my Discovery Person's right knee.*

Could my particular set of empath gifts make it easier for me to know that information is about my partner and not about me?

A. Yes. Back when we surveyed your empath gifts, in *The Empowered Empath*, you learned how some gifts show up more like oneness while other gifts are more about intuition. Practice at Skilled Empath Merge will help you to own your empath gifts even more. You will become accustomed to your personal gifts for receiving information.

All information received during the merge part of a technique concerns your partner.

What can help any empath to accept that? Sample the full sequence of techniques as presented in this Program for Empath Empowerment. Going through all that variety will help you to develop a sense of what doesn't change, which includes how you personally experience Skilled Empath Merge.

Q. *Can we reasonably expect that, with practice, we will like all techniques equally?*

A. I sure don't. And I have had quite a lot of practice with all the techniques in this Program for Empath Empowerment.

I think you'll find something similar. Some techniques will come easier than others. Once you have sampled a variety, a benefit of your experience will be choosing your favorites.

Mostly I stick to my faves. But that is now, having gained the full skill set.

Your learning will go faster if you play with every technique and sample a variety of safe methods for doing Skilled Empath Merge. Then go on to choose your favorites.

CHAPTER 11

A Secret Version
of Truth Sight

You meet Brendan for the first time and, for various reasons, you sense that this relationship could be very important.

Could you use some inside information? Well, lucky you, being a skilled empath. You can do the following technique on just about anyone, and without being noticed.

Granted, a few requirements are necessary to make "Incognito Truth Sight" a reliable technique. Awakening Empath, go through the following checklist and proceed with this technique only if you can meet all the following requirements. No cheating, now!

1. A Correct Angle, Fully Frontal

Are you are close enough to take a good direct look at one of these locations on your Discovery Person, either the midriff or the throat, or both? Can you see it from a front angle?

Do not attempt this technique if you will be peering around from the back (or even off to the side). This skill is tricky enough already, a skill that works best without effort.

Official Technique Time is not a good time to be overcoming obstacles. So don't add awkwardness.

2. A Good-Enough Angle Vertically

How about the up-and-down angle? It's okay if you are seated and must look up to see your Discovery Person. Or vice versa.

Likewise it's okay if you are way taller or shorter than your Discovery Person. Long before learning this technique, you had grown to the height you are now. Maybe you are like me, 5 feet, 1 (proud) inch tall. Maybe you are more like my husband, about a foot taller. For us, relative height is a non-issue; we manage to see each other quite well. For a skilled empath doing "Incognito Truth Sight," relative height is a non-issue too.

All that matters is whether you can take a good clear look, for 10 seconds, holding your head at a pretty even angle. Can you move your eyes without lifting up your entire head? Then you're fine.

3. Socially, It Is Okay to Go Incognito

Be realistic, please. When tempted to use this technique, are you on the job or even publically on display? Then postpone this particular opportunity to do empath merge. Find a better time later.

Such as? It might be fine for you to sit in a pew at church and do "Incognito Truth Sight" on the pastor.

Now what if *you* are the pastor, in full view of everyone? However, the choir is performing now and you're just standing off to one side.

Nope. Although you may not be active right now, you're hardly invisible to that congregation. Don't go weird on them.

Consider this rule of thumb. If you have an obligation to anyone socially, never sneak around while you're with them, multi-tasking in consciousness as if they were too stupid to tell. You wouldn't steal in other ways, so don't steal a few seconds to sneak around researching people while you're ostensibly doing something else.

Admittedly, a little lighthearted spying might not seem to imperil you in any way. You might tell yourself, "I'm in the background now. And I'm fully prepared to drop my empath merge instantly whenever needed."

Hold on. How would you monitor when social *anything* is needed? Only through divided attention during Skilled Empath Merge, which can wreck a perfectly good technique. Avoid developing bad habits that can limit your development as a skilled empath. Instead, simply choose an appropriate time for techniquing. Protect your emerging skill. And speaking of multi-tasking...

4. While You Fly in Spirit, Avoid Multi-Tasking

Multi-tasking is a great art form of our time. You take your everyday waking state of consciousness and stretch it thin while playing with widely different activities. Fun!

Only not okay while pursuing any technique for Skilled Empath Merge. You're not just sneaking a glance unofficially, like admiring a cute guy's looks. Awareness — a singular, effortless, and undistracted awareness — makes empath merge powerful.

By not multi-tasking, you communicate inwardly. Doing one thing at a time, you strengthen your full power of consciousness. You are learning how to direct that consciousness appropriately.

Effortless though "Incognito Truth Sight" can become for you as a technique, that ease does not make the technique trivial. Don't inadvertently disrespect Skilled Empath Merge by treating it like one more way to multi-task.

5. Choose a Discovery Person Who Is Sober

Far as you know, your Discovery Person is not drunk or stoned on recreational chemicals, right?

Unless you are a very, very experienced practitioner of Rosetree Energy Spirituality, avoid doing empath merge or aura reading on anyone who is high. This would make you vulnerable to certain kinds of astral-level STUFF. Protect your energy field.

6. Count This Exploration as Official Technique Time

Awakening Empath, you're still keeping that daily Technique Time to 20 minutes maximum, correct?

Include your time for doing any Skilled Empath Merge. From the first step of your technique to the last step, all of that time counts. Don't stop keeping track just because, "This is fun. And fun shouldn't have to count for official anything." Or other very understandable excuses.

Sure, it can be tempting to slip-slide into techniques. As an unskilled empath, you were perpetually doing Split-Split-Second Empath Merges. You may even have done innumerable Prolonged Empath Merges every day.

After taking months to cease and desist, you have managed to sort your waking hours into:

- Regular time, for positioning consciousness in ordinary human ways (with empath gifts OFF)
- Or your official time for personal development — 20 minutes straight or 5 minutes in the morning plus 15 at night — or however you set up that day's Official Technique Time.

Awakening Empath, count this discernment as a huge achievement in your personal growth. And congratulate yourself for finding a key to successful living in this new Age of Energy.

Nonetheless, you still have a back history when it felt comfortable and consequence-free, vaguely drifting into unskilled empath merges. Which is why I'm gently reminding you: Keep to your current regimen.

Eventually it will feel so comfortable, living with empath gifts routinely turned OFF. And then you will have the basis for fully savoring your delightful 20 daily minutes of Official Technique Time.

It will feel so natural... this amazing, empowered life. A life where it is huge fun to include techniques for Skilled Empath Merge. Among those techniques, "Incognito Truth Sight" is so delightfully portable and varied.

Practice the Position

For this technique you can assume the position without having to request any formal permission of your Discovery Person. Still, you need to get that position right. For practice, look at your Discovery Person and aim your eyes squarely at the ribcage area.

Can you see that part of the body reasonably well? Then you're fine.

Look away. Consider your practice successful. You will know how to "Assume the position" at the appropriate step in the technique that follows.

Will you need to gather your usual recording equipment? Not for an incognito technique! In that regard you will proceed a bit differently.

Technique. INCOGNITO TRUTH SIGHT

Awakening Empath, you have set aside the time, prevented distractions. Plus you have practiced the position. Preview the steps and you're good to go.

1. Sit or stand inconspicuously. Think: "Technique begins." Close your eyes.

2. Gently pay attention to yourself in an easy and casual way. Be especially interested in your emotions right now. Inwardly name one or more emotions. Thinking this counts as the "Before Picture about Your Emotions."

3. Turn attention to your physical body. Notice how any random part of your body physically feels right now. Mentally put a name to this "Before Picture about Your Physical Self."

4. Get Big.

5. Set an intention (e.g., "I am ready to learn about this person").

6. Take three Vibe-Raising Breaths. Immediately return to normal breathing.

7. "Assume the position," aiming your Truth Sight Research Tool at your Discovery Person's ribcage area. After you have connected in this way, let your eyes close. Gently explore what it is like to be you, plus whatever thoughts and feelings you have about your Discovery Person, etc. (All of this counts as information about your Discovery Person.)

8. Find some words to summarize what you experienced. Name it to yourself mentally.

9. Repeat Steps 2 and 3 to mentally record your "After Picture."

10. Think something like, "Hooray, I did great!" etc. Definitely include "Technique complete." Open your eyes and return to "Being normal."

Well done, Awakening Empath! You are back to being normal, all empath gifts turned OFF. As time permits, think about what happened during that Skilled Empath Merge. How about your Before-and-After Picture? And what did you notice about your Discovery Person? Trust it all.

Whenever you do a dedicated technique for Skilled Empath Merge, you add to your cumulative learning and skill as an empath. So congratulations, regardless of whether your findings seemed like a big deal at the time.

Q&A. Incognito Truth Sight

Q. *That was so much fun. I learned a lot about my Discovery Person. But how can I tell for sure if what I found is true?*

A. You can't. Skilled Empath Merge is not scientific. Over time, you will learn to trust the truth value of your experiences.

Suppose that you have done "Incognito Truth Sight" on a new friend, Roxanne. As you get to know her better, notice what she says and does in objective reality.

Later, compare that with your findings from the empath merge. Does it match or not?

As you gain experience with Incognito Truth Sight, you will find that you become extra-perceptive about people. All the while you're remaining yourself, with an ever-stronger sense of identity.

This can be helpful for your friendship with Roxanne, especially that last part. Ideally any technique for Skilled Empath Merge will combine usefulness along with your personal growth, your being a well-balanced person who has a strong sense of identity.

Q. *I didn't see anything. I didn't see colors, which is what I expected. What good is truth sight if it doesn't make you see the colors of the person's aura?*

A. Why do I call it "Incognito *Truth Sight*"? Because this technique launches you into Skilled Empath Merge through *looking.*

As for the results, you could call what you just did "Truth Knowing" or "Truth Feeling" or "Truth Hearing." The point of this technique is an inner knowing, not psychic development or flashy visuals.

And just to clear up another point of possible confusion, aura reading never has to involve seeing colors. That's why it's called "aura reading," rather than "color seeing." Gathering information from a person's energy field is the point, right? Equating information with colors is obsolete in today's world, where success is within reach for everyone who wishes to develop full energetic literacy.

Q. *After I started this empath merge, it did seem to me like maybe my Discovery Person was drunk. But I wasn't sure, so I continued. Now I feel icky. What would you recommend if this kind of thing were to happen in the future?*

A. First, don't blame yourself for selecting a Discovery Person who turns out to be drunk. A surprisingly large portion of the population is high on something. Even when not technically high, plenty of folks have recreational substances left in their systems from last weekend or whenever.

Better to avoid doing Skilled Empath Merge with anybody immediately tipsy or with an ongoing substance dependency (so far as you're aware). And no, you don't have to inquire in advance!

Worldly experience can help you to spot substance use. Haven't you learned some ways by now, like checking pupil dilation or listening for slurred speech? You can use that as a screening technique to avoid doing "Incognito Truth Sight" on somebody under the influence.

Common sense about where you are and who is doing what — that can also help with your discernment of potential Discovery People. If you're at a party where alcohol and drugs are not available, you might discretely seek out some candidates for this technique. If it's mostly a stoner gathering, don't bother.

Q. *Can you recommend other likely places to find somebody sober for my Incognito Person?*

A. You might find a great Discovery Person during work hours. At work. Especially if you are "lucky" enough to work in one of those offices with glass walls, or no walls, between desks. Set the scene properly, of course. Like you're on break, and you're holding a mobile phone (turned off) to one ear.

Or you might sit in a theater audience, watching a performer who is doing something that requires concentration like acting, ballet, or classical music. These artists are less likely than other performers to be playing around with recreational substances.

It's especially fascinating to do Skilled Empath Merge on an actor, in a live performance, whose role demands appearing to be drunk. Such a delicious contrast between surface-level appearance and energetic reality! For this empath, researching someone like that feels a lot like being tickled.

Q. *So okay, I take reasonable precautions but then I start getting this weird feeling anyway. Like what happened to me before. What do you recommend I do then?*

A. Do "Emergency Disconnect from Skilled Empath Merge," which you learned right after "Deep Listening," right at the end of Part One of this book. Here we are now, nearly at the end of Part Two. It's the perfect time for a review.

Also, now is a good time to be reminded that all Skilled Empath Merge is done at your discretion. If you feel strange for any reason — or for no reason — end an ongoing empath merge immediately. Go straight over to "Emergency Disconnect from Skilled Empath Merge."

It's a shame you suffered that short time of feeling weird. But I wonder if it has occurred to you. These days, don't you spend a lot less time feeling weird than previously, as an unskilled empath?

Your feeling weird, and *noticing*, and then being able to stop the empath merge at will.... You might count that as a minor miracle. At the very least, trust that this new freedom of yours is one of many protections built into any Skilled Empath Merge.

Because what is true of this Program for Empath Empowerment? Whenever you fly in spirit, it is now conscious, voluntary, and built around using a specific technique.

Above all, what is your choice now as a skilled empath? You always get to decide whether or not to do an empath merge.

As your skill level develops, this choice will become as clear to you as using a light switch on your bedroom wall. That physical switch has just two positions, either OFF or ON. And who owns that metaphorical version of a light switch? It is you, Awakening Empath.

Q. *While practicing the position for "Truth Sight for Advanced Empath Merge," I was struck by your saying it wouldn't be necessary to formally request any permission before doing it. Now I'm worrying. Ethically don't I always need to ask permission?*

A. When you read a street sign, do you pause to ask permission? When you watch the expression of a stranger in a crowd, without first begging permission, does that count as committing a sin?

I don't think so.

Skilled Empath Merge is a form of energetic literacy. You're learning about somebody, not performing brain surgery or swapping around energies.

Q. *Doesn't it change another person's aura though, using energetic literacy?*

A. A reading is not a healing. That's the sensible way to understand anything that you might do with another person related to auras.

So here is the practical question to ask yourself: Are you using a technique for healing or not?

Aura healing requires permission. Aura reading doesn't.

With all respect, the way you are worrying now could be considered pretty ironic. Previously you used to do unskilled empath merges without once asking permission. And nobody was harmed (except, to some extent, you). Now, doing a short-term empath merge, in an altogether different fashion, it's very sweet that you have developed this concern.

Don't worry. No empath merge changes another person, long-term. Neither a Skilled Empath Merge nor an unskilled one.

I'm so glad you asked about this. Skilled Empath Merges are not only ethical but big, big fun. Amazing education, really. Plus a limitless resource for your personal growth.

PART THREE

Remote Empath Merge

This Empath Empowerment Program has been coaching you to make such progress in your personal development — gentle yet amazing. Let's pause to celebrate that, Awakening Empath!

Part One in this book helped you to consolidate your skills at keeping empath gifts turned OFF, which automatically enlivens your sense of self.

That's a delightful aspect of becoming a Master Empath, incidentally. You can expect your sense of self to keep growing. This will allow your consciousness to become increasingly fluid while you purposely fly in spirit.

Does that combo sound paradoxical? Really it isn't. What's the fun of flying a kite if you don't tether it firmly with a human hand?

Thank you, Awakening Empath, for waiting until you were ready to start exploring Skilled Empath Merge. You did that in Part One via "I Want to Hold Your Hand." Following that, you started to use your first Research Tool, your Deep Listening Ear, as a way to explore other people. With both techniques, your consenting Discovery Person was right there with you in the room.

In Part Two, your mastery progressed. Awakening your Truth Sight Research Tool allowed you to initiate Skilled Empath Merge visually. You even learned your first *incognito* technique, flying in spirit without having to directly ask permission of your Discovery Person.

Now you're ready for even more discreet exploration anonymously. REMOTE EMPATH MERGE means doing Skilled Empath

Merge whenever you please, with whomever you please. Who needs to know what you're doing? Not a soul... except you.

So now, in Part Three, I will introduce you to Remote Empath Merge. These techniques will allow you to learn about anyone. In depth. Through a photo or video; via webcam, through any TV show or movie.

Living today, let's face it. Many of your near ones and dear ones may not live under your roof. By 2012, over 50% of American adults were living alone. The trend is similar in many other nations.

For that matter, do all your close friends live nearby? They might live an hour's drive away, even on another continent. It's great to Skype them or email or text. Yet sometimes don't you long to get closer?

Today's rapid growth in technology can connect us in certain ways. Not all ways, though. When you yearn for true intimacy in close friendships and family ties, high-speed connectivity can't fully satisfy.

If the people you love live far away, you can't smell them. No cuddles. Nor exchanging a manly slap on the back. Except, ha! Once again, you can thank your lucky stars that you were born an empath.

Awakening Empath, it can satisfy a deep yearning for closeness, doing techniques for Remote Empath Merge. You can draw close in consciousness, wherever you live and whenever you like, day or night. Equally important, you can fly in spirit both safely and effortlessly, bringing that jolt of closeness on demand. It is so very human to crave that.

Will these new techniques for Remote Empath Merge become your favorite part of our Program for Empath Empowerment? Find out.

CHAPTER 12

What You Can Bring to Remote Empath Merge

Never throughout human history has it been so easy for people like you and me to know so many people. But know them how well? Today it's common to settle for stunningly shallow relationships.

On a typical day, you see images of how many random faces, 5,000? More? Add to those superficial encounters all the other strangers you stumble upon. The inescapable crowd includes present and former politicians, professional athletes, countless singers and dancers and comedians; actors and models.

To that total, add the folks glimpsed in group audience shots, thousands at the Superdome or a rock concert. How many "extras" have you seen without ever really seeing a single one?

And what do these multitudes have in common? You met them, alright. Only you met them remotely, via a photograph or digital recording, perhaps over your favorite electronic device.

Living today, you know innumerable people in that wide-and-shallow way.

Social networking brings a similar kind of hollow thrill. Following and being followed on Twitter? That can console a person who is otherwise not so well connected, as if quantity really meant the same as quality... to your heart.

In your lifetime so far, Awakening Empath, you have witnessed technological upheavals at a pace unprecedented in human history. All those techno-changes aren't done yet.

Have there ever been so many empaths on earth at one time? Probably not. We 1 in 20 are needed now, I'm convinced. One reason is that we bring a depth to life, a depth that is conspicuously lacking from so much of pop culture during this transitional era.

Yes, I'm convinced that you in particular — you, Awakening Empath — will bring something important to this world every time that you do Skilled Empath Merge. Admittedly, you are using Technique Time this way for very personal reasons, perhaps seeking a deeper human connection or self-realization. Or maybe, simply, delight.

Automatically, though, without your making any extra effort to ameliorate life on earth, you are bringing depth into COLLECTIVE CONSCIOUSNESS, the field of awareness which unites all human beings, present, past, and future.

So long as you confine your explorations to no more than 20 minutes each day, every Remote Empath Merge can help you evolve. Meanwhile you will enrich group consciousness as a side effect. Not too shabby!

Success For You Directly, Not Just Remotely

In our upcoming techniques for Remote Empath Merge, you will start to reach out differently. No more grabbing your Discovery Person by the hand. So it's reasonable to wonder, can you trust the insights from a remote technique?

Really the process isn't so different from doing Skilled Empath Merge with somebody right in the room. Start with an appropriate technique, bolstered by your usual willingness to experiment. Curiosity has brought you this far. Now it can help you to succeed at Remote Empath Merge.

As a skilled empath, what does success mean, anyway? What you learn informs your relationships, helping you to deepen them as desired — one of the greatest interpersonal forms of success you could wish for, right? Additionally, in the background, you are gaining a cumulative wisdom.

One sign of success is your awakening sense of self. This helps you to choose *when* to fly in spirit, plus *which* Discovery Person to select. With Remote Empath Merge becoming feasible, your timing matters more than ever — quite a contrast to the sad old drip-drip-drip of "Perpetually available for unskilled empath merge."

Easily, now, you can alternate growthful, purposeful experiences (occasionally) with empath gifts OFF (habitually). Imagine, exploring life from your own perspective. Imagine, a healthy back-and-forth between discovery and integration, all based on your say-so. In its quiet way, that can be such a big deal.

Because your sense of self is growing stronger by the day, it has now become appropriate for you to use some Technique Time for *Remote* Empath Merge. Every technique you will learn is designed to activate your full gift set for deeper perception. Here I am not referring to your gifts as an empath but, rather, to other ways that you are wired to receive deeper perception.

Your Personal Gift Set for Deeper Perception

Did you know that your inner software includes a full set of inner languages, or PERCEPTUAL GIFT SET, for reading life deeper?

Definitely.

The catch is that all people do not respond to the same inner languages. If you ever study the system of Aura Reading Through All Your Senses®, you will discover fascinating ways you are set up internally to explore life's hidden truths. What matters most in this Program for Empath Empowerment? It boils down to one word: Synesthesia. (Pronounce that sin-ess-THEEY-zhah, not SIN-as-Thee-sia. Joke!)

SYNESTHESIA is available to you, just like every other empath. Non-empaths possess it too, only here's a secret. We empaths can have more fun with it.

What does synesthesia mean? Deep senses working together. Your perceptual gift set for reading life deeper includes many individual gifts. At best, all those gifts work synergistically. Well, synesthesia is what makes those gifts work cooperate so automatically.

Why bring up this technical concept about the nature of Skilled Empath Merge? To give credit where credit is due. Also to relieve you from self-consciousness about the process that will be used in one technique after another. It's reassuring to know that you will automatically benefit from synesthesia.

What else helps your gift set to work? Every technique for Skilled Empath Merge includes "Assume the position." Have you noticed?

"Assume the position" will be included, as well, in all our future techniques for Skilled Empath Merge. Whatever that physical position, it moves your consciousness in a particular way. That specific position plugs you into another person's energy field through one or more of your inner senses.

- With "I Want to Hold Your Hand," it was clairsentience, the subtle sense of touch.
- With "Deep Listening," you used clairaudience, subtle hearing.
- While "Truth Sight" techniques employed clairvoyance, subtle seeing.

Your personal gift set for deeper perception may include clairsentience, clairaudience, clairvoyance, and many other possible gifts.

"Possible" because you don't necessarily have any one particular gift for deeper perception. What matters instead? Your gift set is complete. Some of your gifts will be stronger than others. Definitely, synesthesia will be included, helping you immensely.

Just one measly gift set, per incarnation. That's all I get?
Accept that, Awakening Empath. The collection you were given
can turn glorious when used with skill.

Some aspects of life are non-negotiable. Your personal perceptual
gift set is one. No amount of fussing will change it.

Therefore, Awakening Empath, you might as well relax about your
personal gift set. Since you have already been born, now is not the
time to negotiate. Trust that you really do have a full assortment,
and it is perfect for you. All that you need. Available for you to use
for the rest of your life, effective immediately.

Beware any teacher who asks you to supposedly "improve"
yourself by trying to "develop" a gift that isn't a big deal in your
personal collection. That would be like "strengthening" your body
by trying to make yourself taller or shorter. Find a teacher who
respects you as an individual, including your magnificent gift set
for deeper perception.

Because of synesthesia, what will happen immediately after
you move into a deep level of experience through one of your
perceptual gifts? Automatically, all the rest of your gift set will
activate. That full gift set of yours supports every technique for
Skilled Empath Merge, whichever physical position is used in that
particular technique.

Maybe it makes sense now: Ever wonder why, so far, you found
some techniques more enjoyable than others. Why did one technique yield richer experiences? Or feel more natural and enjoyable
to do? Or just plain fit you better?

The nature of your personal gift set, that's why.

Expect that to continue. You will always have preferences related
to your perceptual gift set.

For developing mastery as an empath, it is especially useful to
experiment with a variety of techniques. Experience will reveal
what fits you best.

For that reason, I recommend that you give a chance, at least once, to every technique in Part Four. It's like shopping for a great new look.

Say that you're in a favorite store where some new styles have come in that season. How can you tell what will look good on you? Try it on.

Self-authority works most reliably after you have given that new clothing — or technique — a chance. Let your process of mastery continue, Awakening Empath.

CHAPTER 13

Remote Empath Merge While Watching TV

Only experiment with this technique if you have already mastered another skill set called "Watching Television."

Similar techno-skills count too, like "Watching YouTube" and "Watching that Streaming Show on a Screen."

What, Awakening Empath? You have met this requirement? You have been doing this kind of perceptual work since you were tiny? Perfect.

Ever worry that you were wasting time with all those electronic amusements? Not so. You could consider it perfect preparation for an amazing form of Remote Empath Merge.

In this chapter I will introduce you to one of my favorite techniques for Remote Empath Merge with an outstanding performer, whether an actor or singer, musician or dancer.

Select Your Discovery Person Wisely

An inexhaustible array of celebrities awaits you. Selecting candidates for Remote Empath Merge, how many celebs can you name off the top of your head?

I suspect that, in all human history, there have never been so many newsmakers, famous politicians, remarkable artists and performers, celebrated athletes.

Many of them are standouts energetically, too, which has helped them stand out in their highly competitive business.

Among them, which will you choose? Context can help you choose wisely.

- ⟿ Exploring the energies of someone you admire, or used to admire, while being interviewed during a scandal? Not such a great idea.

- ⟿ Instead you might prefer to do Remote Empath Merge during a sitcom, a dramatic movie that isn't freakish, a televised concert or dance performance, a wacky variety show like "Saturday Night Live."

Besides your chance to choose a relatively upbeat context, there's a bonus for selecting a Discovery Person who is a performer. After flying in spirit, you can reflect on the information. Then you can compare the performer in role versus that performer's own self, beneath that role.

Doing this about consciousness, not the usual celebrity gossip? Sure. With practice, celebrity watching becomes absolutely fascinating, a unique form of fun for skilled empaths.

- ⟿ You may choose to watch a reality show or talk show with an engaging performer who has intrigued you. What makes that celebrity tick? Find out, you consciousness watchmaker!

Just put all theories aside while doing your aura-level research.

- ⟿ Sometimes you can even do Remote Empath Merge on an athlete — although this is trickier, for technical reasons about "Which Image" that will be explained soon.

- ⟿ Doing Remote Empath Merge with politicians is another superb possibility with the technique you're about to learn.

Personally, I think that Remote Empath Merge before big elections is an empath's civic duty (along with staying reasonably well informed about current events in objective reality). After you have done both, go vote.

So many celebrities! So little time! Choose wisely from all that abundance. And please choose just as wisely when selecting your image for flying in spirit.

Which Image?

After choosing your Discovery Person, you will need to select one particular image to launch you into flying in spirit.

Grab a still shot, rather than a sequence that shows a performer in action. Fortunately, it is quite easy to record a show and then pause it. Experiment, play-and-pausing, until one frame becomes your electronic image of choice.

Why go to that little bit of bother? During our next technique, "Truth Sight for TV," your eyes will look at that image for 10 seconds or less.

However brief that time period, your image must hold steady in order to start you traveling in consciousness. Can you guess all five reasons why?

1. Distractibility

Choosing one fixed image will protect you from getting distracted. Long before engaging in this Program for Empath Empowerment, you learned to watch visual media in the usual way. Now you have something old to unlearn, as well as something new to learn.

For Remote Empath Merge you must learn to *not* watch images as though they were moving. We're so used to rapidly changing visuals on TV shows and movies — probably shot with multiple cameras. Often the sequence of visuals has been edited to move super-fast, all movement and flow, each camera angle rapidly morphing into the next.

Even when you are a very experienced Master Empath, it would be distracting to view a show in that usual way while attempting to research a performer's deepest Otherness.

Remote Empath Merge requires that, if anything, you become more protective of those few precious moments while you are flying in spirit. Why dilute your experience by moving wide, on the surface of images that parade in sequence, grabbing attention at the surface of life? Instead, an empath relishes depth exploration. And that requires no distractions.

Right now, Awakening Empath, you may be wondering how you can learn to watch a screen image without following plot. Without getting caught up in drama. Without being manipulated by a performer's expressions. Well, when following the steps in "Truth Sight for TV," you will be doing exactly that something different. I'll coach you.

2. No touching

Your Discovery Person cannot be shaking hands or patting another person's shoulder.

Also out: No cuddling a baby. No stroking a cat. Although holding a musical instrument would be okay.

For the purpose of Remote Empath Merge, why disqualify someone touching... well, anyone? Every sentient being has an aura. Significant energetic interactions can occur, even during the most casual touch.

The purpose of flying in spirit is to learn as much as possible. One person, not touching others, has plenty to teach you, trust me.

If you are interested in researching interactions at the level of auras, choose a different kind of deeper perception. Aura reading would be a better way to go; I can teach you plenty of cool techniques for energetic literacy, in person, from photos or while watching TV. Just not now.

3. Expect that, energetically, performers change extra fast

Awakening Empath, I don't need to tell you how much life can be crammed into a few consecutive frames. You used to do Split-Split-Second Empath Merges, remember?

Each one took way less than a minute. During that same teensy fragment of time, any human can change drastically at the level of energy. Well, professional performers tend to change way, way more than other people.

The better your skills with Remote Empath Merge, the more confusing it would be for you to string together a series of these depth changes. Still shots are the way to go.

4. Different visual requirements from the usual

Screen directors win prestige for good reason. Any broadcast projected onto a screen, or streaming into your home, had better cram every second with visual interest.

Even the simplest news broadcast or talk show contains multiple strategies to keep the viewer engaged. For instance, have you ever noticed how often a TV news anchor will change position and shift facial expression?

Try watching one of your favorite screen performers with the sound off. Count aloud how many seconds elapse before the chin tilts, the head shifts ever so slightly towards the left or right, eyebrows raise, etc.

Waiting for moments of immobility, you won't reach too many "Three Mississippi's."

Part of a TV performer's talent is to make those incessant physical movements appear smooth and natural, not just plain twitchy. Similarly the vocal trick to a broadcast performance includes how to pace speech way slower than normal, yet make it sound natural.

Accepting illusions like these? You learned to do that back in childhood. Learning to sit down and watch, you were educated to string together all those rapidly moving images on a screen and interpret them as directed.

By now, you don't think twice, probably. The actors sell it. You buy it. In theory, you know that all the images are moving very rapidly. In practice, you sit and watch, entraining with whatever you are being shown.

A Nielsen report at the end of 2013 calculated that American adults spend 11 hours a day connected to digital media. That doesn't include media time at work, either. Very likely, you have developed a huge appetite for electronic viewing, complete with a subconscious craving for ever-new camera angles and turns of the body.

Besides that, you have been coached to ignore a performer's facial characteristics, like large chin thrust or a nose angling strongly to one side or one eye higher than the other. Tricks of the visual trade, like clever camera angles, have manipulated your emotions or pulled you into preferring an MTV-like parade of contexts, moving faster than humanly possible.

Watching those streaming images, it can feel as though you have dual citizenship. Sometimes human. Otherwise living on a parallel planet. Earth-like, this surreal world has accustomed you to find normal human interactions quite bland by comparison.

Until now, anyway. Behold! A new skill set awaits. Awakening Empath, you are going to learn how to use electronic images instead of being used by them. (Or, to be more accurate, instead of being used by the people who make money by keeping you hooked on various broadcasts.)

"Truth Sight for TV" will embolden you to control the use of electronic images, doing it your way, and in a more selective fashion. For your purposes as an empath, what won't you need? Rapidly moving, fresh new versions of a face.

Also, you will need images that show more than a talking head. At a minimum, for most techniques, choose an image that includes your Discovery Person's whole neck. And for the technique I'm about to teach you next, that image will ideally go at least down the ribcage to the midriff area.

5. Camera angles do matter

What if you were drinking whiskey with the goal of getting as drunk as possible as fast as possible? You might order your drink "Neat," with no diluting chunks of ice or other liquids.

Likewise, when you do "Truth Sight for TV," order your image straight up. This will allow your awareness to fly as deeply as possible, as clearly as possible.

Pause your sequence of electronic images until you arrive at one that is fully frontal, where your Discovery Person shows from face to waist — or at least down to the midriff area — clearly visible with no effort from your part. So very suitable for Remote Empath Merge!

Practice the Position

Awakening Empath, now you understand all five requirements for selecting a suitable image. Before you learn how to use it, go get that image of your choice and return for our next step of techniquing.

Which physical position will work best when you do "Truth Sight for TV"? Position yourself so that you can see the image you have chosen, see it right on the level, see it easily and comfortably.

What else? Depending on the device used for your image, it might need to be refreshed from time to time. If so, practice doing that reflexively right before you "Assume the position." Including right now, at practice time.

Now for your official practice: Aim your Truth Sight Research Tool at your Discovery Person's midriff area. Can you see it reasonably well? Then you're fine.

Look away. Consider your practice successful.

Automatically your eyes will revert to everyday uses. Yet thanks to that simple practice, you will know how to "Assume the position" at the appropriate step in the technique that follows.

Before your Official Technique Time begins, what else? As always, take precautions to prevent interruptions. Silence electronic devices that won't be used to do this technique. Ask roommates to give you some space. Temporarily banish all pets from the room.

What can stay in that room with you? Besides your electronic image, keep your recording equipment handy, whether a favorite digital recorder or dependable, low-tech writing equipment.

Technique. TRUTH SIGHT FOR TV

Awakening Empath, now you're ready to fly in spirit. You have set aside the time, prevented distractions. Recording equipment is handy, and you have practiced the position. Preview the following steps in advance of doing this technique. Then let's go already!

1. Think: "Technique begins." Close your eyes.

2. Gently pay attention to yourself in an easy and casual way. For the moment, be especially interested in your emotions. Inwardly name one or more of them. Doing this counts as a "Before Picture about Your Emotions." Open your eyes long enough to record a quick summary; then close eyes again.

3. Turn attention to your physical body. Notice how any random part of your body physically feels right now. Put a name to this "Before Picture about Your Physical Self." Open your eyes long enough to record a quick summary; then close eyes again.

4. Get Big.

5. Set an intention (e.g., "I am ready to learn about this person").

6. Take three Vibe-Raising Breaths. Immediately return to normal breathing.

7. "Assume the position," aiming your Truth Sight Research Tool at your Discovery Person's ribcage area. Keep eyes open for a minute or less, according to what feels comfortable to you. Then let your eyes close. Everything you experience now will inform you about your Discovery Person in the here and now. So let yourself notice whatever you notice, whether it seems to be about yourself or your Discovery Person. All thoughts, feelings, images, textures, etc. count as information about your Discovery Person.

8. Find some words to summarize what you experienced. Open your eyes long enough to record a quick summary and then close eyes again.

9. Repeat Steps 2 and 3 to record your "After Picture." Remember to close your eyes after recording.

10. Think something like, "Hooray, I did great!" etc. Definitely include "Technique complete." Open your eyes and resume "Being normal."

Look over your findings. What was the impact on you, doing this technique on this particular occasion? What did you learn about your Discovery Person?

Only then resume watching TV. Although you might want to stop and practice an audition for your fictional reality show of choice. I recommend "Dancing with the Stars Who are Empaths." Because if your Discovery Person was a dancer, you did. You danced in consciousness.

Q&A. Truth Sight for TV

Q. *I think I'm in love. This technique was made for me. My two favorite things are empath merge and watching TV. Is it possible to do this technique too much?*

A. Unless you enforce smart time limits, yes, it could definitely be tempting to overdo.

Look, it can be a thrill to safely fly in spirit and learn about your favorite celebrities. Even a mediocre TV show can yield fascinating experiences. Just remember the context, your life. Including your sense of identity.

Collecting empath merge experiences is not like collecting shoes. Your consciousness is involved. So avoid losing your sense of proportion. It may help to remember the difference between quality time and quantity time.

Go for quality. Limit the quantity.

Q. *I'll be honest with you. I can't think of anything more interesting than finding out what makes my favorite celebrities tick. So far, I have done everything in your Program for Empath Empowerment just as you asked. It helped, believe me.*

Now I'm worrying. Maybe I have opened up something scary big with this TV technique. What if I get into binge-watching, only it isn't watching one series on the outside but watching actors from the inside, like for hours? How can I keep from going overboard?

A. Such a smart question. It would not be responsible to turn empath merges into a way of life. But you're in control of you mind. And your schedule. So fear not.

Just remember your priorities. Long term, you are strengthening your sense of identity and moving forward on your path of personal development. That is the uniquely thrilling drama.

Entertainment is not the only purpose of a human life. Watching regular surface-level TV can be so enticing. Clearly you haven't yielded to the temptation of excessive screen time. Otherwise you would not have made it this far into our Program for Empath Empowerment.

Avoid losing yourself in the glamour of empath merge. For a skilled empath, the ultimate entertainment is your human life. My recommendation to you? Research no more than three celebrities in a day. Short times and superbly done!

Q. *I'm annoyed about how you have tried to limit us about "Select Your Discovery Person Wisely." What's the point of self-authority if I can't decide for myself which shows to watch and then fly in spirit? I happen to like thrillers. It's only movie violence, not real. What's wrong with doing Remote Empath Merge on any actor I like?*

A. As a process, Remote Empath Merge protects you from taking on Imported STUFF. However, you will be strongly influenced subconsciously by the content of every empath merge.

What is wrong with exploring the chief suspect in the latest murder controversy? Not the *process* of flying in spirit but the *content* of information being received. By definition, every empath merge gives you direct and deep experience of what's like to be that individual at that time.

Common sense will, hopefully, remind you that everyone on TV is not an appropriate Discovery Person. Choose wisely.

Q. *I'm not trying to be difficult, just honest. What if the only people who interest me are the rebels and mavericks?*

A. Tastes can change. When you continue to grow as an empath, what will you value? Could be, you'll develop a new kind of taste that delights you, even while supporting your personal development.

For now, let inspiration be your guide. Inspiration, not shock value. Especially when selecting a Discovery Person, choose somebody who is personally interesting to you in a positive way. Even a little bit interesting? That will be fine for starters.

Many of us have no idea of how warped our tastes have become, due to the media's desperate search for market share. The nature of screen time today is to exalt the unusual, the weird, the gossipy and petty, the pathologically strange. Exalt how? By calling it "Brave" or "Rebellious" or "New and interesting."

Sure, some folks enjoy this parade of ever-escalating craziness. As more STUFF is stuck in their auras, only horror will make much of an impression. If you now suffer this degree of energetic clog, I would recommend some sessions with a professional at Rosetree Energy Spirituality. STUFF can always be healed.

Yet probably what you are asking about is far easier to change. Just undertake a conscious experiment. Purposely counterbalance that socially-induced, habitual taste for variety.

One day at a time, how about this? Allow yourself a few moments to explore a tender form of experience that has a more positive inner impact. Remote Empath Merge is the opposite of channel flipping by a jaded viewer.

Choosing to live this way could make you a pretty counter-culture sort of rebel, actually.

CHAPTER 14

A Handy Tool for Remote Empath Merge

The price for this next Discovery Tool is a bargain. You already own it.

Except probably you haven't been using it for the purpose of launching a Remote Empath Merge.

What is this tool exactly? Your hand. More accurately it is one of your hands. That hand becomes a full-fledged Discovery Tool when used in a dedicated technique for Remote Empath Merge. This flexible tool, used for remote exploration, can produce superb results.

You see, Awakening Empath, everybody has one hand that works especially well at receiving information energetically. Let's call this your **PRIMARY SENSOR HAND** or **TRUTH-TOUCHING RESEARCH TOOL**.

Your other hand is a **POWER HAND**, ideal for *sending* energy. Favor that hand if you do healing work in a form of energy medicine like Reiki.

In your role as skilled empath, however, what matters more is *receiving* information in the form of energy. Frankly, you will be receiving a kind of information that can rock your world.

It is an amazing privilege to do Skilled Empath Merge, even while in the same room with somebody else. Soon you will not be limited to researching people in the same room as you. Not when you can learn a variety of techniques for Remote Empath Merge.

Which is why you may find it thrilling to discover how one hard-working hand of yours, already useful for so many other purposes, can help you to succeed as an empath.

Which hand will serve as your Truth-Touching Research Tool? Let's find out.

Technique. LOCATE A HANDY TOOL FOR REMOTE EMPATH MERGE

Awakening Empath, you have set aside the time, prevented distractions. You have previewed the following steps in advance of doing this location technique, which will be super-quick. So you're good to go.

1. *Interlace your fingers.* Clasping your hands together, palms touching, one pinky will be lowest followed by the other, then one ring finger, and so forth.

2. *Wiggle whichever thumb is on top.* Now raise the hand attached. It is dominant for you, which is why it counts as your Power Hand. Is it left or right? Make note. Then interlace your fingers again.

3. *Wiggle the thumb that lies underneath.* That belongs to your Truth-Touching Research Tool. Duly make note and maybe add a little dance of jubilation. Definitely stop interlacing your fingers. Usually they work better separately.

Make mental note of this Truth-Touching Research Tool. This will serve as your Discovery Tool for Remote Empath Merge, employed for many techniques in this Program for Empath Empowerment. Sweet!

Q&A. Locate a Handy Tool for
Remote Empath Merge

Q. *When I interlace my fingers, I am very proud of the fact that I automatically keep both thumbs side by side. Does that mean I am twice as powerful an empath as ordinary people?*

A. Funny you! It means that you are so busy being proud of your dexterity that you have failed to notice your other fingers.

Easy to fix. Interlace your hands again. Which pinky lies on the bottom? The hand attached to that is your Truth-Touching Research Tool. Use that hand for certain techniques of Remote Empath Merge.

Q. *I have always heard that your right hand is for giving energy and your left hand is for receiving energy. Can't I just go along with that instead?*

A. Sure you can. Except, wait. Do you mind sacrificing results?

Whoever passes along generalizations about "Everyone's" right hand has probably not stopped to do much teaching of empath-related techniques. You can find many popular energy techniques, over-simplified to help everyone to participate and enjoy some kind of feel-good experience.

A free-and-easy experience worth how much? Maybe not so much.

You're invited to benefit from my rigor when helping people, effectively coaching individual empaths around the world.

Avoid mix-and-matching any part of this Program for Empath Empowerment with other ideas or approaches, even if they appear similar. I have been working in mind-body-spirit since 1970. You can be sure that I have encountered all the popular clichés about energy, this one included. If I do not choose to retweet them, it is for good reason.

Q. *Since I have two hands, why not use both of them? Won't I get twice as much information?*

A. Not recommended. If you were to use both your Truth-Touching Research Tool plus the Power Hand, you would get two different sets of information... plus a generous helping of confusion.

One of your hands specializes in sending energy while the other specializes in receiving it. Therefore, the quality of perception differs. Neurophysiologists could probably map this on your brain. Outside the lab, humble common sense explains it pretty well: Instead of going back and forth between two very different streams of information, flow with one stream.

Simple is good for any technique for Skilled Empath Merge. Remote Empath Merge, especially, is complex enough without making it unduly hard on yourself.

CHAPTER 15

Truth-Touching Empath Merge

In our latest technique, you will be using your Truth-Touching Research Tool to plug into your Discovery Person's energy field, then enter with your consciousness. Not physical touch. More like having your hand serve as a launching pad to fly in spirit.

So far, this Program for Empath Empowerment has taught you how to use Truth Sight, a visual tool, for Remote Empath Merge. Now let's bring on the Truth Touching!

Just as you are wired to have one hand only as your Truth-Touching Research Tool, and one Deep Listening Ear, you are wired to prefer either vision or touch as a basis for Skilled Empath Merge. (To prefer at least somewhat, and maybe to strongly prefer.)

CLAIRSENTIENCE is the fancy name for Truth-Touching, just as clairvoyance is woo-woo-speak for Truth Sight and a third metaphysical name, CLAIRAUDIENCE relates to your Deep Listening Ear. Awakening Empath, have you guessed? I prefer more down-to-earth terms for these universal human abilities.

Still, those clair-words can be fun to use. Really, isn't it fascinating to think that you could have something in common with Joan of Arc? She's the uneducated peasant girl who famously heard voices that led her into battle. Victoriously!

Although credited for the French victory over the British at Orléans, Joan was later burned as a heretic. Still later, she was canonized by the Catholic church. So much drama need not accompany your subtle senses, including clairaudience, clairvoyance, and clairsentience.

Which will give you better results for Remote Empath Merge, Truth Sight or Truth-Touching? Don't be so sure you know the answer quite yet, not until you have explored a variety of techniques.

What have I noticed, teaching workshops? Many of my students assumed (incorrectly) that they were more clairvoyant than clairsentient. Really, why wouldn't folks assume that seeing matters most? Today's society and technology are strongly visual. Just think of the beautifully designed range of i-Products.

Living now, Awakening Empath, you are sure to use your eyesight a lot. Notice, we speak of "Watching television" because that sure isn't "Listening to the radio." Yet your inner wiring for deeper perception may not emphasize seeing over hearing or touch. Quite possibly, Truth-Touching serves you better as a launching pad to fly in spirit.

Which will prove to be stronger for you, Truth Sight or Truth-Touching? In this part of the Program for Empath Empowerment, let's experiment. Learn how to do a Remote Empath Merge by using your Truth-Touching Research Tool. Find out how much fun that can be. Save your comparisons for later. (Please reserve the right to be surprised.)

Refine Your Selection of Discovery Images

For this TV-based technique, you will choose one particular electronic image. Only let's refine that a bit. Here come some tips to help you attain the clearest experience possible.

1. Start by selecting your electronic device for viewing.

2. Find a good sequence on screen, then pause it to show one frame with your Discovery Person facing you directly.

3. Locate an image where your Discovery Person is not touching anyone else.

4. This image may be larger than the image you used with "Truth Sight for TV." Preparing for this new touch-based technique, it is ideal to work with a close-up that shows

the full face plus the upper torso. Ideally this image of your Discovery Person is nice and big. And aren't streaming videos full of those convenient close-ups!

Awakening Empath, with practice you can work from a smaller image. But larger ones will always be easier. At least they are for me.

If your Discovery Image must be refreshed from time to time, practice doing that reflexively right before you "Assume the position." Speaking of which....

Practice the Position

Now let's practice your physical position for "Truth-Touching TV Empath Merge."

Can you easily and comfortably see your Discovery Image? Move into that convenient position.

Next, practice aiming at the desired body part, your Discovery Person's neck. Can you see it reasonably well? Then you're fine.

Position your Truth-Touching Research Tool at the correct angle, sideways rather than up-and-down. The distance would be about 6-12 inches in front of your screen. Keep your fingers and thumb loosely together, rather than letting your fingers spread apart.

Maybe it will help to proceed as though your fingers are in a mitten, definitely not a glove but a mitten. (And if a mitten had only one compartment, including space for your thumb, that would be even more like this desired Research Tool position.)

Next, Awakening Empath, you have a choice of direction. Will you aim your empath merge tool to the left or right? Choose whichever direction feels more comfortable.

For further comfort, keeping your Discovery Image stationary, you might take a step or two to the side. Also you might wish to adjust how you are bending your elbow. Experiment with these little postural adjustments until you find what feels comfortable.

Congratulations! This way of positioning your Truth-Touching Research Tool can become the basis for good habits, serving you well whenever you use that tool for Remote Empath Merge.

What may vary, from one technique to another? Where your Research Tool will be positioned in front of your Discovery Person's body. This time, of course, it's the neck.

With your preparation complete, look away from the image. Once you stop using your Truth-Touching Research Tool, it will instantly revert to default uses as a regular hand.

What else will help you to prepare before our next technique? As always, take precautions to prevent interruptions. Silence all the usual electronic devices except for what you will need to display your Discovery Image. Ask roommates to not interrupt you. Temporarily banish all pets from the room.

What stays in that room along with you? Besides your electronic image, keep recording equipment handy, whether a favorite digital recorder or low-tech writing equipment. All can be kept within easy reach. Then preview instructions for the technique.

Technique. TRUTH-TOUCHING EMPATH MERGE WITH TV

Awakening Empath, you are totally prepared to "Assume the position" at Step 7, complete the technique and enjoy the insights that result. Go fly in spirit with help from your Truth-Touching Research Tool.

1. Sit or stand near your Discovery Image. Think, "Technique begins." Close your eyes.

2. Gently pay attention to yourself in an easy and casual way. For the moment, be especially interested in your emotions. Inwardly name one or more of them. Doing this counts as

a "Before Picture about Your Emotions." Open your eyes long enough to record a quick summary; then close eyes again.

3. Turn attention to your physical body. Notice how any random part of your body physically feels right now. Put a name to this "Before Picture about Your Physical Self." Open your eyes long enough to record a quick summary; then close eyes again.

4. Get Big.

5. Set an intention (e.g., "I am ready to learn about this person").

6. Take three Vibe-Raising Breaths. Immediately return to normal breathing.

7. "Assume the position" with eyes open for a minute or less. Everything you experience next will inform you about your Discovery Person at the time of the image you're researching remotely. Allow yourself to gently notice whatever you notice, whether it seems to be about yourself or your Discovery Person. All thoughts, feelings, images, textures, etc. count as information.

8. Close your eyes. Stop using your *Truth-Touching Research Tool;* immediately it will revert to being a regular hand. Find some words to summarize what you experienced. Open your eyes long enough to record a quick summary and then close eyes again.

9. Repeat Steps 2 and 3 to record your "After Picture." Remember to close your eyes afterwards.

10. Think something like, "Hooray, I did great!" etc. Definitely include "Technique complete." Open your eyes and go back to "Being normal."

Look over your findings. What was the impact on you, doing this technique on this particular occasion?

And what did you learn about your Discovery Person?

Q&A. Truth-Touching Empath Merge with TV

Q. *Wow, I liked that so much better than using my Truth Sight Research Tool! How did this work?*

A. Your Discovery Person has an energy field, full of information. This is a very real part of the TV image that has been recorded electronically.

Whether you use your **Truth-Touching Research Tool** or your **Truth Sight Research Tool**, combining that with an effective technique will make it easy for you to research that person's energy field.

Whichever tool you use, there will be a Preparation Process to position your consciousness.

At "Assume the position," you will plug in, connecting to your Discovery Person's energy field.

Just follow the rest of the instructions for that particular technique. Automatically you will do safe and informative research into what it is like to be that Discovery Person.

Q. *What do you mean by "Plug in"?*

A. To PLUG IN with consciousness means to actively make contact with somebody's energy field as part of a technique.

To understand this process more vividly, start by understanding yourself. Energetically you are much like a lamp that can plug into a wall socket.

Think of the lamp that you use most at home. All necessary mechanical circuits are built into that lamp. It works great. Whenever you wish to make that lamp work:

- First it must be plugged into an outlet or power strip. Then the energy can flow.

- Next, you use a simple switch... another mechanism built into that appliance.

- On goes the light. Use that lamp.

∼ When you're finished, just turn the switch off. Unplug the lamp. Very energy efficient... and, although your lamp isn't working right then, it's available for future use.

Awakening Empath, in many ways your consciousness works like an appliance, built with an amazing circuitry.

Your consciousness doesn't light things up physically. But can you awaken your consciousness, at times of your choosing. Being a born empath, you are equipped to directly experience what it is like to be another person.

As a skilled empath, you choose when you will turn on that version of lively consciousness that wakes up within the aura of another person.

Engaging with your Truth-Touching Research Tool or your Truth Sight Research Tool, either way, you plug into your Discovery Person's electrical field. Then a dedicated technique actively switches on your flow.

Naturally, with Skilled Empath Merge you are gaining information rather than shining light.

Q. *So, in theory, could I plug in my Truth-Touching Research Tool off and on all day long? Wouldn't that help me to grow faster as an empath?*

A. Quite the opposite. Like any other technique for Skilled Empath Merge, either use a particular technique or keep your empath gifts safely OFF. Definitely count any plug-in technique as part of your Official Technique Time.

Q. *What if I didn't feel a thing? This is just my hand, we're talking about. Even though I used my hand for this technique, weirdly, I didn't feel a single thing.*

A. Actually, that's good. This technique is not about physical touch. You are exploring consciousness *through* your hand, moving into the energy field of your Discovery Person.

Once you get to Step 7, everything you experience is really about your Discovery Person: Your emotions, how you feel in your body, the flow of your thoughts, insights, ideas.

It can take a bit of practice to fully appreciate that no empath merge is physical. With a Remote Empath Merge, even less so.

Q. *Can non-empaths also plug in with a technique to learn about another person?*

A. Yes. Every non-empath can learn plug-in techniques of aura reading. Potentially very insightful!

As an empath, however, you are extra fortunate. Besides being able to learn aura reading, you can do techniques for Skilled Empath Merge. This allows for a deeper kind of exploration.

Q. *Can empaths also learn to read auras, or must we automatically move into Skilled Empath Merge?*

A. Such an important question! Of course, empaths can learn to read auras. However you are fortunate if you are first doing this Program for Empath Empowerment. Otherwise any attempts at aura reading have probably moved you into unskilled empath merges.

When it comes to reading auras, all systems and techniques are not alike. Be discerning about the method you choose. For example, the system of Aura Reading Through All Your Senses® is designed to be safe for empaths, as well as non-empaths.

Q. *Say that I am a skilled empath — which I guess, by now, I am. What would be different for me, doing aura reading versus Remote Empath Merge?*

A. That depends on which system of aura reading you choose. Much in the field of deeper perception is psychic work, whereas the aura reading I teach is a form of energetic literacy.

Say that you study with me and are doing a technique for aura reading. You will receive information, just like a non-empath. By contrast a technique you learn here for Skilled Empath Merge will highlight your deeper abilities for experience.

In this Program for Empath Empowerment, you get to choose whether or not, according to common sense, it is safe to do a Skilled Empath Merge. What a difference from those old, whatever-ey, perpetual in-and-outs with your consciousness.

Here is a personal example. When profiling celebrities at my blog, I usually start with a bit of aura reading, just to find out if I like that Discovery Person. Just because someone is talented or famous doesn't mean the person's consciousness would be a treat for me to experience at depth.

I am extremely selective, choosing when to seek a more personal experience through Remote Empath Merge.

Q. *I enjoyed the Truth Sight technique so much more than this one for Truth-Touching. Shouldn't I be able to enjoy them both equally?*

A. Not at all. Most empaths prefer either to plug in through touch or to do research through sight. Although some of us have a mild preference, other empaths discover a preference that is very strong.

I'm one of those empaths with an extremely strong preference. In my case, it's for using Truth-Touching rather than Truth Sight.

Having a strong preference is no limitation. That's simply how I'm wired, along with everything else about my personal gift set as an empath. If you have a technique preference, same deal.

Q. *It so happens, I'm a perfectionist. I'm used to working on problems until I can master them. How long will I have to work before I will like the Truth-Touching version just as much as the other kind?*

A. Since you would be wasting your time, I can't begin to give you an estimate. Even as a perfectionist, you have only one head and two eyes. Is that also something to "Work on"?

Even perfectionism has its limits. My advice? At this time in your life, do not use Truth-Touching techniques. Choose Truth Sight instead.

Q. *Do you think I'm like the guy who just asked the last question? Is it necessary for me to make this kind of choice? Will I have to commit to just one type of technique for the rest of my life? What if I liked them both?*

Here's my problem. I liked Truth-Touching quite a bit, but I must admit that Truth Sight is more of a favorite.

A. Only specialize if you have a strong preference. In your case, make your choice in the moment, as you prepare for any remote techniques in the future.

That one specific time, choose either Truth Sight or Truth-Touching. Stick with your choice while doing that particular technique on that particular occasion.

First time you do our next technique, for instance.

CHAPTER 16

Remote Empath Merge
with Photographs

I may be prejudiced about this. But as a big fan of the Harry Potter books and movies, I think that doing Remote Empath Merge with a photograph is just as good as those magically alive pictures at the Hogwarts School for Witchcraft and Wizardry.

Plus it's real, not fictional.

And pretty darned convenient, as well. To use the photo-related technique in this chapter, all you require is a regular muggle photograph or digital image, no magic wand required.

Seriously, Awakening Empath, have you ever counted how many pictures you see every day? To do all that counting... could practically take you all day.

Let's do something way more informative, and start reading some of those pictures. I mean reading pictures as never before, moving you toward a new level of mastery as an empath.

Wouldn't it be amazing if you could safely fly in spirit toward your choice of people in photographed images? That means everything from an heirloom daguerreotype of bygone relatives to the selfie you took just yesterday to show a new friend.

The technique is effortless, once you practice a little. So here comes one of my favorite discoveries for Skilled Empath Merge, presented to you for the first time as "Remote Empath Merge Through a Photograph." This is a remote technique that you can do with people who are not just celebrities. Bring on Remote Empath Merges with real people, the ones who matter most in your life.

*Yes, you're learning how to gather inside information
for love, business, and friendship.*

Choose a Smart Photo

Surely you have heard of "Smartphones," Awakening Empath. Advanced technology to some of us these days! (At least when first publishing this book in the winter of 2014.) Well, Smart Photographs for Remote Empath Merge will require no technology beyond your discernment.

That discernment begins with intelligent selection of your Discovery Person. Decide. Do you really wish to experience this particular person so directly, at depth? Don't just be honest. Protect yourself.

Discernment can also help you to choose a suitable photo... for your purposes. You will be researching your Discovery Person at the time of the photo. To learn about a 30-year-old you are interested in dating, don't go for a baby picture.

Enticing adult photos, also in birthday suit? Not recommended. It's best not to forge a subconscious association between sex and exploring another person's energy field.

Will it matter whether the photograph of your choice is print or electronic? Not one bit. Just make sure that you can see your Discovery Person clearly. And from a front angle.

Depending upon which technique you'll be using for that Remote Empath Merge, your picture may need to extend all the way to the start of the legs. Sometimes, though, a simple headshot could be plenty. For instance while doing our next technique: A headshot that includes the neck will be fine.

Definitely make sure the entire face shows, though. Sometimes it looks cute to crop an image mid-forehead. Personally, I find it unsettling to use that kind of photo. Ugh! I prefer to experience the person with a head that has not been sliced off, even somewhat.

Preferably several inches of space are visible above the top of that head. (To me, doing an empath merge, that feels like "breathing room.")

Now, you might feel more comfortable than me that way, but why bother to find out while you're first learning how to do the technique? For your first time with it, the point is not how hard you can make things for yourself. Quality information matters more. What helps make that happen? The ease of your process.

Speaking of which, beware choosing an image where your Discovery Person is touching a person or pet. (This will be my last reminder about this, Awakening Empath. You're strictly hands off now, etc. Automatically. Always. Right?)

Well, now that you know all the useful particulars, I will start calling this suitable kind of picture by a new name. Your DISCOVERY IMAGE.

That means a well-chosen photograph or a still shot from a video or electronic device, an image suitable for Remote Empath Merge.

Practice Positioning Your Discovery Image

Now for practical considerations related to *using* that Discovery Image for Remote Empath Merge. Will you be holding a hardcopy photograph or an electronic device? Either way, you have considerable leeway in how to position things physically.

Awakening Empath, I want you to enjoy maximum ease and flow during every single Skilled Empath Merge. Your success will never be just about talent. Skill matters. Making yourself physically comfortable can become a routine part of your skill.

By referring to "Discovery Photos" and "Discovery Images," I hope to instill new habits, quite different from the usual ways you play with photographs. A Master Empath needs expert positioning skills, effortless and well suited to Skilled Empath Merge.

For starters, find a way to hold your Discovery Image at eye level, as though your Discovery Person were sitting right there in front of you.

While sorting out these logistics, also find a super-convenient location for the materials to record your findings with the technique. Such mundane skills of preparation! Yet they are essential for success with the fancier part, your experience of Remote Empath Merge.

"Practice the Position" for the technique that follows? It comes down to this:

- ∼ At Step 7, starting the merge part of your technique, you will pick up this photograph or electronic device, holding it at eye level.
- ∼ If you will be using your Truth-Touching Research Tool, hold the Discovery Image with your other hand.
- ∼ Alternatively, if using your Truth Sight Research Tool, you can use either or both hands for holding the Discovery Image, whatever feels comfortable.
- ∼ Avoid any temptation to let your photograph or device lay flat, like on a table.

Practice now, picking up and holding your Discovery Image. Move it to the height that brings your Discovery Person comfortably close to eye level. Make that neither too close nor too distant.

Experiment to find comfortable angles for using your eyesight, your hand. That is the YOU part of the equation. The full equation goes like this:

Good Discovery Image + YOU + Technique =
A successful Remote Empath Merge

Always position your Research Tool at a particular body part of the Discovery Person. That's the TECHNIQUE part of the equation. It's also wise to physically practice your position for using your Research Tool. So that comes next.

Position Your Research Tool

Hello, mouth! That's your plug-in location for this upcoming technique. For your purposes, it doesn't matter whether your Discovery Person's mouth has been photographed speaking or silent, smiling or in repose. Even if mostly covered by facial hair, no worries. Just aim in the general vicinity.

Awakening Empath, this will be your first technique for Remote Empath Merge via photo. Variations that you learn later can include different locations for researching, but your Discovery Person's mouth is definitely the one to use this time.

- Your Truth-Touching Research Tool will be held horizontally as usual. Center your palm over the Discovery Person's mouth.
- If using your Truth Sight Research Tool, aim it so that your Discovery Person's mouth is the focus of your vision.

After you practice "Assume the position," look elsewhere. Or, if you were using your Truth-Touching Research Tool, let it drop down.

Awakening Empath, usually one quick practice of "The Position" is all you need before leaping into the fun part of a technique. Since this is your first time doing Remote Empath Merge with a photo, let's add just a bit more preparation to help you establish good habits.

Photo Finesse, Depending on Technology

How you position your Research Tool may vary, depending on the type of Discovery Image you have selected. For each option, a bit of tweaking can help to refine your skill for flying in spirit.

A hard-copy photograph

Keep that Discovery Photo physically separate from other pictures that you might have lying around.

What if your Discovery Photo is lying on a table? While doing your Remote Empath Merge, remove other random pictures from that table. In no way do you want to be distracted. Commit to researching one special photograph at a time.

A picture in a book, magazine or newspaper

Fold pages, or turn them, until only one picture shows at a time. Make sure it can be seen easily. Manage that along with holding up your Discovery Photo at a good angle.

A framed photograph, hanging on a wall

Granted, wall decorations can be a bit tricky. Position either yourself or the picture so that you can comfortably see the face at eye level.

If using your Truth-Touching Research Tool, how can you position it appropriately? Practice in advance of doing the technique, no matter how experienced you become at Remote Empath Merge.

If you can't make your choice work comfortably, seek a different Discovery Image. (Yes, ease and comfort matter that much.)

An image via your laptop or other computer

To avoid distractions, close all other windows and turn off incoming messages. In everyday life, you may be used to multi-tasking or being interrupted. You may adore being connected, constantly available to friends who reach out. Well, not now, please.

Doing Remote Empath Merge, you will be moving your consciousness in a different way. Protect the integrity of your experience.

Support your screen on a table, not your lap. Sit facing your computer and check the relative positions of yourself and whichever image you'll use as a launch pad for flying in spirit. Maybe you will need to prop up your device. (Right now I'm using a couple of low-tech books to raise my computer monitor to eye level.)

Practice "Assume the position" with your Discovery Tool.

An image via your tablet or smartphone

Practice holding your Discovery Tool at eye level. Make sure you have a table or the equivalent within easy reach. Note: Your lap is never an appropriate location while doing this technique.

If your electronic device must be refreshed from time to time, practice doing this automatically at the start of "Assume the position." Make this a habit.

Okay, Awakening Empath, now you are properly prepared. So worthwhile investing the time! This new technique may become the one you use most often as a Master Empath.

Technique. REMOTE EMPATH MERGE WITH A PHOTOGRAPH

Awakening Empath, you have practiced the position with your Discovery Image. And you have set aside the time, preventing distractions. Recording equipment is handy. Just read through these instructions as a preview. Prepare for success!

1. Think: "Technique begins." Close your eyes.

2. Gently pay attention to yourself in an easy and casual way. For the moment, be especially interested in your emotions. Inwardly name one or more of them. Doing this counts as a "Before Picture about Your Emotions." Open your eyes long enough to record a quick summary; then close eyes again.

3. Turn attention to your physical body. Notice how any random part of your body physically feels right now. Put a name to this "Before Picture about Your Physical Self." Open your eyes long enough to record a quick summary; then close eyes again.

4. Get Big.

5. Set an intention (e.g., "I am ready to learn about this person").

6. Take three Vibe-Raising Breaths. Immediately return to normal breathing.

7. "Assume the position," focusing on your Discovery Person's mouth. Keep your eyes open for a minute or less, then let your eyes close. Meanwhile ask inwardly, "What is it like to be this person?" Everything you experience next is information that counts about your Discovery Person at the time of the image you are researching.

8. Find some words to summarize what you experienced. Open your eyes long enough to record a quick summary. Then close eyes again.

9. Repeat Steps 2 and 3 to record your "After Picture." Afterwards remember to close your eyes and finish this technique properly.

10. Think something like, "Hooray, I did great!" etc. Definitely include "Technique complete." Open your eyes and go back to "Being normal."

Look over your findings. What was the impact on you, doing this particular technique on this particular occasion? What did you learn about your Discovery Person?

Q&A. Remote Empath Merge through a Photograph

Q. *Why use the mouth, of all places, as my entry for Remote Empath Merge?*

A. Compared to staring in real life, photo reading can make it far easier to gaze at somebody's mouth or place your hand sideways in front of that rather personal body part.

For research purposes, you might consider this location a delightful, ethical new way to snoop extra effectively.

Of course, every time you fly in spirit now, you're gaining fabulously useful information to help you in love, business, and friendship.

Q. *What if you don't notice anything in particular, either by looking or touching?*

A. No problem — just keep yourself open to receiving information whenever you do this technique in the future. It might take a few explorations with different Discovery People and their photos. Soon you will grow comfortable with this latest technique for Skilled Empath Merge.

Q. *Can I use a portrait for a Remote Empath Merge?*

A. Never. Paintings, even genius works of art by great masters like Leonardo da Vinci or Rembrandt, do not contain a person's energy field. By contrast, photographs and electronic images capture all the info automatically.

How convenient for us empaths! We can get great results with ordinary pictures. No need to purchase original Rembrandts just for research purposes.

Q. *What's the point of keeping my eyes open when I am using that Truth-Touching Research Tool? I wasn't seeing much of the photo. Mostly I was seeing the back of my hand. Why not just keep my eyes closed?*

A. Keeping eyes open means that your consciousness is directed outward, towards your Discovery Image. In this technique, using the option of the hand-based tool, it doesn't matter what your eyes physically see.

That's right, it doesn't matter in the least whether your vision makes contact with a hand or the photo.

What does matter? That your hand — as a Truth-Touching Research Tool — is positioned appropriately. At the same time, having your consciousness directed towards your Research Image (because your eyes are open), now that's the desired combination.

Q. *I'm still confused. While doing your technique, I'm seeing the wrong thing and that's supposed to be okay?*

A. If you're strongly visual, this explanation I've just given may seem confusing. Not to mention doing research with that Truth-Touching Research Tool, where it bothers you to be seeing your hand more than the photo.

Whereas if you're strongly kinesthetic (geared toward truth-touching), you may never have noticed that you are, literally, seeing your hand while in technique. (Until you asked this question, this had never once occurred to me. After maybe 10,000 times using my Truth-Touching Research Tool. Pretty funny, actually!)

Awakening Empath, however you are wired with your perceptual gifts, choose the Research Tool that you find works most comfortably. By now, you can choose to always go with either the vision-related tool or the hand-related tool. And what if you're comfortable with both? Lucky you! Choose one tool for one technique at one time and the other at a different time.

Just because all you Brave Explorers are empaths does not mean that you have identical gift sets for deeper perception.

Q. *I found a photo that met all your requirements. I used it, no problem. But are you seriously going to tell me that you are quite so strict yourself when choosing a photograph?*

A. When you are very experienced, you may bend the rules just a bit. Admittedly I do, after decades of experience. Almost never, though. And I do a lot of professional work that requires Remote Empath Merge.

Despite all that experience, I still prefer using a photo that's simple to access. It is just plain harder, working with a picture that was taken at an odd angle. Effort and strain never help an empath, regardless of how experienced you become at Skilled Empath Merge.

Q. *Come on, don't you ever do Remote Empath Merge on somebody who is holding hands with somebody else, or that kind of thing?*

A. I am much more strict about physical contact than any of the other rules I have given you for photo selection. So that means really, really strict.

Energetically, people vary a great deal in how they interact with others. Some stay separate, though touching. Others move into full-blown unskilled Empath Merge or other ways of mingling energetically.

This is particularly fascinating with actors during a performance, because a love scene can include two actors who are completely ME-focused. Or sometimes one actor strongly connects to the other actor, while that second actor remains oblivious, stunningly self-absorbed.

In short, my advice is to avoid doing Skilled Empath Merge on people who are physically touching. That includes Remote Empath Merge using photos where people hold hands, lean in to bump shoulders, etc.

If I wish to learn more about what is going on with these people, I prefer to substitute a technique for aura reading. The process is simpler than a Remote Empath Merge.

Alternatively I will find a photo with those same folks when they are not physically touching. Then doing individual empath merges becomes easy.

Have you noticed? One of the themes in this Program for Empath Empowerment goes, "Why give yourself a hard time?"

Q. *The skeptic in me has to ask, how can I know for sure that I'm really plugged in?*

A. Along with the skeptic grumbling inside you, every empath has a trusting voice. That part of you already knows the best answer to this question. While in technique, choose to trust.

When you dip your hand in water, it will get wet. Surely you don't keep examining your hand to reassure yourself, "Ooh, is it really wet?"

Similarly whenever using the technique presented here, know that the Preparation Process prepares you well. Know that. Trust that. You have been readied, in abstract consciousness, before plugging into your Discovery Person's aura with your research tool.

Each dedicated technique for Skilled Empath Merge works automatically. You are plugged in. Knowledge flows. You record it. Review your notes afterwards, not while in technique.

What will happen if you make an extra effort to push away doubts about whether yes, you are plugged in really, truly, for sure? You can push yourself right out of the spontaneous experience.

Q. *How can I turn up the volume for that trusting voice?*

A. Place zero emphasis on whether you're getting good results. Just in that moment, add one of the techniques from your Preparation Process.

Yes, every technique in your Preparation Process can be used extra times, as needed, during the empath merge itself. Choose any one you like to keep yourself in flow.

For instance, what if you have a moment of doubt at Step 7? Technically this comes after your Preparation Process, right? Well, just sprinkle in two extra Vibe-Raising Breaths. Or you could repeat your intention. Or Get Big again. Then resume whichever technique step you were doing.

Another kind of confidence comes from using your techniques for Skilled Empath Merge when it isn't an abstract exercise but done for a practical purpose. How can you use the techniques in this Program for Empath Empowerment... in order to improve business relationships, friendship and love?

CHAPTER 17

Love, Business, and Friendship

Let's take a moment for gratitude. Celebration is richly deserved. You have mastered Remote Empath Merge. From now on, any appropriate photograph can be used for insight into a person of interest to you.

You may even have begun to appreciate that remote techniques are no harder than doing Skilled Empath Merge with somebody physically there with you in the room.

Speaking of which, a person in the room with you *can* be the object of an Incognito Empath Merge. More to celebrate!

Yet the in-person empath merges can be big fun too. Many a friend or date may be intrigued at the prospect of Skilled Empath Merge, provided you ask first. Then bring on "I Want to Hold Your Hand" or "Deep Listening." You can fly in spirit in a big way, visceral and bouncy and sometimes quite startling. Awakening Empath, you're so skilled now, you can do more than celebrate. It's time to start calling yourself... a Master Empath.

What Does It Really Mean, Being a Master Empath?

Your human life is precious to you, based on a strong and positive sense of identity. Now your life story has one main hero, YOU. When you face problems, as all mortals must, you will say things and do things... at least if you aim to get results in objective reality. That's a far cry from traveling within other people's energies, idealistically searching for clues that will, supposedly, produce results in objective reality.

Now you use your words. You do things, not just know things. And when you wish to know deeper, you can use empath talent and skills to do that very effectively.

Accordingly, life has become your playground; effectiveness brings you confidence. It is a thrilling cycle of personal growth.

Yet your desire to know more about people hasn't gone away. To satisfy that, a Master Empath uses up to 20 Daily Minutes of Official Technique Time. On any given day, some or all of that goes towards Skilled Empath Merge.

As a Master Empath, you've got skills now. Nothing about your empathic exploration depends upon *chance*. Instead you have *choice*.

Will it be Remote Empath Merge through a photo? How about Incognito Empath Merge with somebody in the room? Or, this time, do you prefer to do a Skilled Empath Merge with a consenting Discovery Person?

Your choice. Your chance to explore Otherness and deepen your experience.

Exploring is safe for you, always, since the rigor of well-designed techniques will minimize the risk of Imported Stuff.

As a Master Empath, you decide when and why and how to fly in spirit. Whichever technique you choose from this Program for Empath Empowerment, you will succeed. There will be soul-stirring surprises and, sometimes, inspiring discoveries.

Use your skills for fun and profit, your way. Bring it! A Master

Empath's advantage for love, business, and friendship.

CHAPTER 18

Five Extra Apps for a Master Empath

Life is rich for a Master Empath. You can celebrate Empath Empowerment in so many ways. Inside information is yours for the asking. Fun!

Indirectly, your status as a Master Empath can also increase your success. More getting what you want when it comes to love, business, and friendship — and why? Long before gaining your awesome empath skills, you were already an interesting person. Well, now you have extra insights to share as you discuss business colleagues, books or movies, enjoy closeness with special friends, reach out through technology. Small talk can grow just a bit bigger.

Ironically, Master Empath, you may also find it easier to talk with non-empaths.

Come to think of it, aren't you having fewer thoughts like this? "If Justin really cared about me, he would understand me better."

You know better now, right? Non-empaths can have great depths of caring, yet that doesn't allow them to become empaths. Caring won't change a person's natural fingerprints, either.

Certain distinctions are becoming crystal clear: *Non-empath* versus *unskilled empath* versus *skilled empath*.

For example, you may find it easier to enjoy when caring, perceptive non-empaths struggle to piece together their theories about what makes other people tick.

Sometimes these folks will, clearly, be projecting. With all respect, some of those theories might be pretty lame. In the past, this might have confused you. Now it's easier to accept.

Empaths are born with at least one talent to directly experience with it is like to be other people. Other folks are born with different talents. That simple.

You can't squeeze blood from a stone, but from that same piece of rock you might squeeze out a sense of stability.

Another example: Some non-empaths will develop a perfectly valid understanding of mutual friends or business associates, bringing a perspective that would not have occurred to you. It's an outsider experience, yet nicely done. In contrast to the inside experience that *you* are free to have as a Master Empath. Which can be nicely done and ha ha! Effortlessly mega-perceptive.

Well, relax and enjoy it.

The Golden Part

In short, the *content* is thrilling. Your insights as a Master Empath can give you a huge advantage at friendship and love; business, too.

More subtle is how much you can grow spiritually from the *process* of directly experiencing Otherness. This is truly a golden knowledge.

Exciting though it is to live during today's age of rapidly developing technology, no electronic invention can match a skilled empath's access. Technology delivers quality information about objective reality only. A skilled empath can plumb the depths of subjective reality. Not all the time, but during Official Technique Time. And at will.

As you live the implications of this, you will glimpse a thrilling potential for improving your life further. Among other things,

Master Empath, this Program for Empath Empowerment is allowing you develop a very refined kind of restraint.

Sure, techniques for Skilled Empath Merge are the fun part. Meanwhile, maintaining your quality of life will depend upon, mostly, keeping your empath gifts turned OFF. Through consciousness. As a matter of habit.

It's up to you now. When will you decide to do your next Skilled Empath Merge? And then, how will you use that golden time?

To get you thinking, here are five of my favorite apps for Skilled Empath Merge. May you discover many more!

1. The Birthday App

How lavishly do you celebrate your major birthdays? Or your minor ones?

Already you may value birthdays as important celebrations of your unique and precious human identity. Well, from now on, each of your birthdays can include:

- Celebrating your achievements over this past year (or past decade).
- Setting meaningful goals that match your current desires.
- Gratitude for your favorite things, whatever they may be at this time in your life.
- Acknowledging how much you have grown inwardly, personally, spiritually.

And for the last of these, of course, nothing beats a Skilled Empath Merge.

Starting with this next birthday, you might make it an annual custom to take a pair of photographs. Either take a selfie or have somebody take both these photos for you.

Fascinating Photo #1

What is the essential picture to take every birthday? Not the cake!

Capture an indispensable Discovery Image for your collection as *a skilled empath*. Get yourself a fully frontal, tastefully dressed, photograph that extends from your head to your legs.

Then you can do Skilled Empath Merge on that new, improved version of yourself.

Comparison research is the really fascinating part. Line up one or more birthday photos from previous years. Research each one in the same way, making a record of your observations. Then compare your results. Maybe write that down, too.

You will flesh out fascinating details about your personal development, one year at a time. Compare that to some bland, wishy-hopey sentiment like, "You're not getting older. You're getting better"!

Optional possibility: Fascinating Photo #2

A clear, annual mug shot can become the basis for some powerful *face reading*. What, assess meaningful changes to your facial characteristics? Hello! That's today's leading edge of the 5,000-year-old art of reading faces for character.

Once you develop a good skill set for physiognomy, you will want to document your evolving face every year.

Reading your face for character can reveal a hidden world of meaning. Indirectly, face reading can also protect your self-esteem, giving you the power to smash illusions that limit how most adults see themselves. An annual mug shot can help you to value new physical changes, specific ways that your spiritual growth now outpictures facially.

Either you can learn face reading for yourself or you can go to a professional face reader who will interpret how your soul expresses in your evolving face. What won't you be able to do? Time travel back, year by year, to take a simple mug shot every birthday.

If you own a home, you probably change your smoke alarm batteries once a year. That's smart, protecting yourself. Smart in a different way is to take a good clear annual photo of your face.

Why pay more attention to your smoke alarm (or haircut, or clothing) than to your highly significant, spiritually meaningful, once-in-a-lifetime physical face. Well, you can change that, starting now.

And a final possibility:

The Ultimate Annual Birthday Self-Research

If you do write down a face reading to supplement your Skilled Empath Merge, then you can go one step further in self-validation.

Empath merge supplies one level of truth while physiognomy provides different insights. Compare and contrast.

To tie up this gift with a bow, record these observations as you go. Now that's a real keepsake, year by astonishingly growthful year.

2. The Parenting App

Are you a parent? Then you won't want to miss out on this app for Skilled Empath Merge.

Of course, let's define "Parent" loosely. Let it include raising one's biological child, being a step-parent, foster care arrangements, the unique love of a grandparent or great-grandparent, getting involved as an aunt or uncle, even volunteering as a Big Brother or Big Sister. Or, in business, when you give back by mentoring.

Yo, parenting person! Do an occasional Skilled Empath Merge on that kid. Learn inside-out what is happening with your child.

Among other reasons to do some discrete detective work: You can screen for the use of alcohol or pot. Remote Empath Merge could be less awkward than a full-out search of your child's room or mobile phone, don't you think?

Look, it's only fair. Your child has home turf advantage, combined with kid wiliness. By contrast, you happen to be a Master Empath.

Do I recommend that you explain to your child about your doing those surveillance-style Skilled Empath Merges?

Okay, you can stop laughing now. Has your child ever used the phrase "Too much information"? As a Master Empath, give yourself permission to take responsibility in this manner.

You can do your Skilled Empath Merges discretely, supplementing all your other good parenting skills.

3. The Emergency Kit App

Master Empath or not, you can't predict what will happen at wacky Earth School:

- ~ Speaking of parenting, as we were before, it can be a huge adjustment to become an empty nester.
- ~ Other kinds of death are more literal, and you can't opt out of real-life consequences as simply as, say, silencing your mobile phone.
- ~ Jobs can be lost, or money, or carefree physical health.
- ~ Work changes might disrupt your career. Or you might take the initiative to find a new line of work. (Even when you make career changes by choice, that seldom makes a new path easy.)
- ~ Love affairs start or end; marriages, too.
- ~ How refreshing when you can celebrate a relationship that stands the test of time, a major anniversary!

Situations like these deserve the special kind of upliftment that a Master Empath can provide. Use a recent photo (or Annual Birthday Photo) for a Remote Empath Merge.

This can remind you of who you are, how distinctive you are, and how strong you are. Or help you to revisit the best in those you love.

4. The Gift App

Master Empath, if you love your friends, don't spoil them. Especially don't get in the habit of frequently giving them Skilled Empath Merges. Don't keep giving just because you can.

And it's so easy for you, and helpful for them.

Inadvertently this could train your loved ones to expect you to provide on-demand services as an empath. Trust me. This will not end well, over the long term. (As I have learned from personal experience.)

I would like to spare you, Master Empath. Ordinary common sense will tell you that relationships work better with balanced give and take, while services given so freely are not necessarily respected.

What is appropriate, though? What could even be constructive for certain relationships?

Give the *occasional* gift of a Skilled Empath Merge. Give it for a major birthday or an uplifting perspective at life passages. Your insights could really be the best gift ever.

5. The Movie App

Consider this empathic app only if, like me, you really love movies. Then, wow, do you ever have a treat available as a Master Empath!

You can do Remote Empath Merge to evaluate an actor's performance. For years I have done this with Academy Award nominees.

Curious about how deep an actor's performance went? Technically an actor can do a superb job, convincing an audience without changing very much beneath the surface. However, the best of the best really do change all the way down to their who-you-be.

This way to fly in spirit is the ultimate in film entertainment

Every year, I do Aura Reading Movie Reviews. Sometimes I'll do regular aura readings on nominated actors. For my very favorites, I'll do Skilled Empath Merge.

Either way, energetic literacy-based film research is one of the most fascinating things you can ever do as an empath. Here I will outline the technique so that you can start doing it, too.

Prepare for film research as a Master Empath

After the annual Academy Award nominations are announced, decide whom to research. You'll be able to fathom subconscious-level transformations of your favorite nominees for Best Actor, Best Actress, Best Supporting Actor, and Best Supporting Actress.

Once you select the performers who intrigue you, one option is to join the annual conversation at my blog. Or do the research entirely on your own.

Of course, this research isn't just for the Oscars. You can use the following technique for any competition in the performing arts, such as the Grammys or the Tony Awards, where the performer is taking on a role that is supposedly different from regular "Being myself." (No easy job for any A-lister.)

Select your Discovery Images

To explore acting from this perspective, you will need two contrasting images:

1. Find a Discovery Photo or Discovery Image that shows the actor or actress *in the nominated role.* Use a still taken from the film rather than a publicity photograph that was shot separately. Alternatively you might prefer to pause a movie trailer, using what you have already learned about selecting a Discovery Image.

2. You will compare this with a Discovery Photo that shows the actor or actress *while not officially acting.*

For that second option, it helps that celebrities are gorgeously photographed attending award shows like the Academy Awards, plus many excellent photographs can be available at a star's official website.

Search engines on the Internet, like Google images, might be an even faster way to access celebrity images suitable for Skilled Empath Merge.

Just avoid the creepy paparazzi photographs that show public figures at their worst. All of us have off moments; it's ethically inappropriate as a basis for empath merge, and probably not typical of that person, either. Avoid researching anyone's aura at such times.

Say no, when appropriate

When preparing for aura reading movie criticism, bring along your common sense.

Does the nominated role portray violence, abject misery, or other horrible kinds of experience? Avoid doing any technique whatsoever for Skilled Empath Merge. Research a different movie role instead. Why?

Although Imported STUFF is no danger to a Master Empath, skills won't protect you from being influenced by the content of a photo. Subconsciously you could be imprinted with loads of disturbing impressions.

Did you know that your subconscious mind stores all your experiences permanently? It sure does. So don't voluntarily add to your ongoing subconscious storage locker of horrors.

TECHNIQUE. Film Research as a Master Empath

Once you have assembled your pair of comparison photos, research away. Use the same technique, the same Research Tool, for each photograph. Record your research, as usual. Compare the actor's usual way of being to the performance. Deep down, what changes?

Sometimes you won't notice much difference. In that case, blame neither yourself nor your research. Many world-famous actors don't really change much, inwardly, playing one role or another. Some of the biggest stars always play themselves. They win awards for it, too.

Show biz is mostly about the surface of life, after all. Yet some actors transform themselves inwardly, at such depth and with such creativity, it is astounding. It takes a Master Empath to savor this fully.

At my blog, you can read about performers who have received top marks from me for achieving astounding "Chakra Change Points." Here's a short list.

10 Actors to Watch, From Inside Their Performances

1. George Clooney in "Up in the Air"
2. Helen Mirren in "The Last Station"
3. Leonardo DiCaprio in "The Wolf of Wall Street"
4. Meryl Streep in "Julie and Julia"
5. Colin Firth in "A Single Man"
6. Cate Blanchett in "Blue Jasmine"
7. Bradley Cooper in "The Silver Linings Playbook."
8. Anne Hathaway in "Les Miserables"
9. Jeff Bridges in "True Grit"
10. Nicole Kidman in "Rabbit Hole"

Whatever your interests and hobbies, as a Master Empath, you can have enormous fun researching actors during their greatest performances.

CHAPTER 19

The Power of a Skilled Empath

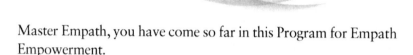

Master Empath, you have come so far in this Program for Empath Empowerment.

You know so much about how to turn your empath gifts OFF. Consequently, you know more than ever about your irreplaceable human identity. Each day you are making delightful discoveries about your human self, expressing a unique greatness. Only you can bring this into the world.

When you decide to turn your empath gifts ON, you can choose from so many techniques that are effective. Meanwhile you keep yourself safe from Imported STUFF. Even as a Master Empath, you can continue to evolve. (For more ideas, turn to later books in this series.)

Mainly, you can safely morph, in consciousness, into the who-you-be of any Discovery Person. As a Master Empath, what will be the sign of your mastery?

Whichever techniques you favor at any given time, you will focus most on your own life.

- How can you guarantee a productive day or week or year? One situation at a time, on purpose, use your empath gifts.
- Use your gifts and skills for love and business and friendship. Gain that inside information and use it to advance your career.
- Or wallow in wisdom for its own sake.
- Or use what you learn to about other people to serve them.

For any purpose that you desire, as a Master Empath, you'll be empowered. Because deep, truthful knowledge really does bring greater effectiveness in life.

Note, too, that a Master Empath does just enough Skilled Empath Merge. Neither too little nor too much. Which helps your life to become just exciting enough!

This Program for Empath Empowerment has brought you knowledge and skills to support your personal goals in life. *The Empowered Empath* got you rolling. And now *The Master Empath* has accelerated your momentum of skill. What remains? To integrate.

Master Empath, may you continue to find abundant possibilities for personal growth and fulfillment. Joyful opportunities abound for you as a skilled empath. You — a complex individual who happens to have talent as an empath! That life as a skilled empath is just getting started, really. Which experiences will you collect along the way?

Collections and Recollections

Memories of favorite empath merges are what I collect now, the way some hobbyists love their coins or antiques.

My older collection, though, is memories of beaches. Since childhood I have treasured those memories: The sound of crashing waves on Sunday mornings at Jones Beach in New York; the wild, southern smell of St. Simon's Island in Georgia; the strangeness of Miami shoreline, complete with those mysterious palm trees; an otherworldly first encounter with the Pacific Ocean.

As a Master Empath, I now have a bigger kind of collection, and you can, too. Whatever else you may like to collect, whenever you purposely fly in spirit, you'll never lack for valuables. More than ever. Deeper than ever. You can collect ways that spiritual beings are human, in all their glorious Otherness.

Some of the memories in your Empath Merge Collection may be sad ones. In mine, for instance, are recollections of my father, Ernie Rosenbaum. Now I appreciate him as one of the most talented empaths I've ever known. Ignorant about his gifts, however, he lived un-empowered by empath talent. He suffered a lot.

In his happier moments, Dad loved music, especially playing music for friends. He volunteered as an empathically gifted disc jockey, finding the musical frequency that would resonate most for each individual. Gleefully Ernie would select the perfect music from thousands of vinyl record albums kept on a huge bookshelf.

Then Ernie would watch how that particular friend would listen and glow up. Meanwhile, I would sit quietly in the background: Watching, doing Prolonged Empath Merges with Dad's friend, then with my beloved father. Meanwhile (as I now realize) Ernie was, likewise, doing a Prolonged Empath Merge on that friend.

At mid-life my father nearly died from a sudden attack of diverticulitis. Recuperating in the hospital, what brought him back to health? It was the musical need of his roommate, a Greek sailor who spoke no English. Ernie vibed out which music the sailor would like, then asked my mother to bring it from home along with a record player. (Yes that's what we quaintly called our technology back in the day.)

Once Dad found the right music, both men healed "in record time." The sailor was soothed by the sounds of home, while my father sailed into his hospital roommate's relief and delight.

But life for an unskilled empath means life on a nonstop journey — now sailing, now diving, now hurtling over a roller coaster. When empaths don't know how to handle all the knowledge that flows through them, it can break their hearts.

I believe this is what happened to my father. He would wake up screaming in the middle of the night, one heart attack after another.

Sure, doctors explained his broken-heartedness in strictly medical terms, a harshly objective layer of explanation.

Although true, that seemed to me a beside-the-point way to diagnose my father's pain. Whatever the cause, increasingly my father came to live in the sterile world of hospitals, with their Latin diagnoses, unnatural odors, and rooms that were mostly walls and sickbeds.

By age 55, Ernie's arteries had hardened prematurely, the doctors said. Senility was just one item on his long list of diseases. Personally, the part I found hardest to take was the loss of his intelligence. Truth to tell, my father could barely think.

When I came to see him for the last time, the look of death clung to him. Ernie had always carried a huge energy field, beaming out a love of life that struck you like an almost physical force. Now he lay in a hospital bed, physically and aurically shrunken. Pitifully small in a faded blue hospital gown, with vacant eyes, he vaguely acknowledged this visitor, his daughter.

In years past I had paid respect to dying relatives, made small like this, tucked like dolls into their hospital beds. This time was different. I was saying goodbye to my favorite relative. Memories could have flooded me with love and wonder, gratitude and rage. Instead I felt empty. All my spiritual beliefs couldn't take away the grim reality of loss. It was very hard to say goodbye.

My mother, who visited every day with what was left of Ernie, tiptoed out of the room to leave the two of us alone.

How could I say goodbye? For once I had no words. I searched. Then inspiration came.

"Dad," I heard myself say. "If we held hands and I meditated, do you suppose that you could feel it?"

He gave a childlike smile. Emotional Oneness was still his favorite thing. I held Ernie's hand, closed my eyes. At that time in my life, I had zero skill as an empath but I was very experienced as a teacher of Transcendental Meditation. So I flew in spirit to the highest heaven I could reach.

My Dad joined me there. I could feel his presence in the twinkling silence. Minutes later I peeked at him and saw him sitting, eyes closed, aurically beaming. It was our last conversation. I left him there.

So many people, like Ernie, slip in and out of deep knowing. But it's never quite conscious. While living that way, they can never claim their full power, neither as empaths nor as people.

Master Empath, your life is going to be very different. Go on, show the world how to be an empath with loving purpose and great power.

Share Your Experiences, Master Empaths

Easy to get and effortless — that's your new flow of information from Skilled Empath Merge. You can do it in person, from streaming images, from photographs. Using techniques learned here, you have so many ways for safe exploring. It's easy, too.

Do you know what can be hard? Getting book reviews.

Here is where you can help, Master Empath. Please write a review of this book, then share it at Amazon.com, barnesandnoble.com, goodreads.com, and any other book review websites you know. Even a couple of sentences can make such a difference for other empaths.

You'll also be giving back to this indie publisher, who strives to bring innovation to spiritual self-help... and always do it with integrity.

What else? As a Master Empath you may start collecting stories, as I do. Well, yours might be perfect for my future books or at the blog "Deeper Perception Made Practical."

I would love to read your tales of triumph and discovery. Send them to Rose Rosetree, 116 Hillsdale Drive, Sterling, VA 20164. Email to rose@rose-rosetree.com

It is so exciting. You are among the first Master Empaths in the world. It has been such an honor to guide you through this Program for Empath Empowerment.

Bring your special wisdom into this world, bolstered by all your skill!

About the Author

Rose Rosetree teaches empaths. This award-winning teacher, the founder of Rosetree Energy Spirituality, wrote the first book in the field of empath coaching, *Empowered by Empathy.*

Among her trademarked systems is Empath Empowerment®, helping empaths to lead more powerful and fulfilling lives. Rose is now authoring a series of books about the emerging discoveries of skilled empaths worldwide.

Her pioneering work with energetic literacy has appeared in 1,000 media outlets, including *The Washington Post, The Los Angeles Times,* "*The View,*" *USA Today* and "The Diane Rehm Show." Rosetree's leading-edge books — 361,000 copies sold — have been published in 13 languages.

CPSIA information can be obtained
at www.ICGtesting.com
Printed in the USA
FFOW05n0400230415